Praise for *Lo*

"A compelling journey—brilliant, poetic and astonishingly truthful—into realms of love and honor where, like Beatrice in Dante's Inferno, this book's guiding hand could be the difference between delight and disaster."

–Timothy B. Tyson, author of *Blood Done Sign My Name*
(winner of the Grawemyer Award in religion)

"Craig Werner and Rhonda Lee have crafted a brilliant study of love, using the seemingly incongruous figures of Dante, Shakespeare, Austen, and Rev. Al Green not only to guide us through central texts but also through our own lives. Kudos to the authors for writing in a style both scholastically substantive yet refreshingly readable! The third chapter offers rich insight into Jane Austen's surprisingly modern treatment of eros and philia in a society where love was a commodity. Jane Austen fans and foes should not miss Werner and Lee's introductory remarks on the manufactured version of "dear Aunt Jane" or their discerning discussions of *Pride and Prejudice*, *Mansfield Park*, and *Emma*. After reading *Love & Happiness*, my eyes have been so opened to the nuances of love that I think I will never read classic literary texts in the same way—nor will I perhaps be the same as a wife, daughter, or sister."

–Emily Auerbach, author of *Searching for Jane Austen* and co-host of "University of the Air"

"Craig Werner and Rhonda Lee have created a stunning success in *Love & Happiness*, walking the razor's edge between creativity and commentary with grace, honesty and dignity. *Love & Happiness* breaks down Big Love into three principal forms: eros, or sexual love; philia, or familial love and trust; and agape, a profound love for all. Using classic literary figures as well as recent soul music greats as inspirational yet conflicted points on their map, Werner and Lee bring these subtexts into a sharp, knowing focus. Shaped by the Christian tradition, moving from Shakespeare to the great Al Green, *Love & Happiness* is that rare thing, a fresh insight into our most studied, primary impulse, Love."

–Stewart Francke, award-winning musician and author of *Between the Ground and God*

"*Love and Happiness* offers a liberating and refreshing look at how eros, held hostage by entertainment media as overly lustful or by conservative politics as inherently shameful, can serve as a powerful creative force that can activate greater intimacy with community, and passion with spirituality. This book dusts off Ancient Greek tenets of love, long forgotten, and remixes them with rich examples from classic literature and soul music. Werner and Lee practice what they preach as their words embody the co-creative potential that lies at the core of every relationship. *Love and Happiness* offers us the key to unlocking mental, emotional and spiritual intimacy in ways that would earn the good Reverend Al Green's 'Amen.'"

–Roberto Rivera, President, The Good Life Alliance

LOVe
&
HaPPiNess

For Eric,
in the spirit
of the 3 lanes.

2/4/15

Eros According to Dante,
Shakespeare, Jane Austen,
and The Rev. Al Green

Love & Happiness

Craig Werner &
Rhonda Mawhood Lee

White Cloud Press
Ashland, Oregon

All rights reserved. Copyright © 2015 by Craig Werner and Rhonda Mawhood Lee. No part of this book may be reproduced or transmitted in any form or by any means whatsoever, including graphic, electronic, or mechanical, including photocopying, recording, taping, or by any information storage or retrieval system, without permission from the publisher.

White Cloud Press books may be purchased for educational, business, or sales promotional use. For information, please write: Special Market Department, White Cloud Press, PO Box 3400, Ashland, OR 97520
Website: www.whitecloudpress.com

Cover and Interior Design by C Book Services

First edition: 2015
14 15 16 17 18   10 9 8 7 6 5 4 3 2 1

Printed in the United States of America

Library of Congress Cataloging-in-Publication Data

Werner, Craig Hansen, 1952-
Love & happiness : eros according to Dante, Shakespeare, Jane Austen, and the Rev. Al Green / by Craig Werner & Rhonda Mawhood Lee. -- First edition.
pages cm
Includes bibliographical references and index.
ISBN 978-1-940468-12-9 (pbk. : alk. paper)
1. Love in literature. 2. Happiness in literature. I. Title. II. Title: Love and happiness.
PN56.L6W48 2015
809'.933543--dc23
                    2014030086

Introduction:
"So I asked the Lord about it…"

The Reverend Al Green bathed the crowd in a smile that took the edge off the unseasonably cold Little Rock autumn night. He'd played a full set and the crowd had sung along with every song: "Let's Stay Together," "Tired of Being Alone," "L-O-V-E," his gospel hit "Everything's Gonna Be Alright," covers of the Temptations' "My Girl," Sam Cooke's "Bring It On Home to Me," and the Soul Stirrers' "Jesus Gave Me Water." At the sound of the straight-out-of-church organ introducing the evening's final number, a wave of joyous anticipation—half sex, half spirit—spread like a wave through clear water. Transforming the concrete amphitheater into an outpost of the Full Gospel Tabernacle he pastored just up the road in Memphis, Tennessee, the Reverend began with a confession: "Sometimes people say I shouldn't play this song…" He stepped back from the microphone to give the good-natured cries of protest time to subside, then went on, "So I asked the Lord about it." A hum of approval urged him on. "And he told me to ask *y'all* how *you* got here." Not waiting for the "amens" to fade away, the band swung into "Love and Happiness."

Everyone knew the song. Male or female; married or single; black, brown or white; straight or gay. Didn't matter. *Love can make you do right, love can make you do wrong.* Judging by the expressions on their faces, more than one listener had stood at that crossroads. They could hear the voice on the phone at 3 a.m. whispering that she, or he, could make it right. They'd lived through the moment when you didn't know whether to come home early or stay out all night long. When you couldn't tell the difference between sin and salvation. When you felt your lips forming the *yes*. But then you heard your heart whispering *no*. You hesitated, thought again. Maybe, like Reverend Green, you prayed—however prayer looks to you.

Like Al Green's song, *Love and Happiness* is a prayer. It's our meditation on love, our appeal for guidance on behalf of a culture that desperately needs it. At the heart of the book is the type of love known as *eros*. Usually understood as sexual desire, libido or sometimes just lust, eros possesses enormous power. It's creative love, which taps into the deepest parts of the soul, inspiring earth-shaking music and art, knitting two people together physically and emotionally to create a home, a family, and a shared history. When eros is warped, bad things happen: its power can destroy lives, spirits, marriages. Being faithful to a higher call, tasting victory, may mean walking away from the voice at the other end of the telephone at 3 a.m. But turn away when you should reach out, and you may be left with the taste of ashes for the rest of your life. In the middle of the night, creation and destruction can be hard to tell apart.

Our goal in writing *Love and Happiness* is to change the way people see eros, and help them liberate its creative power. We place eros in conversation with two other types of love: *philia*, the reciprocal love of friends, family and community; and *agape*, the self-giving love that sustains the world, the ultimate power that people of faith call God. In secular terms, eros is love for one; philia, love for many; and agape, love for all.

Our argument is this: eros has the strongest potential to be a creative force when it's embedded in networks of philia, and suffused with agape. Remembering our bonds with the people in our lives—honoring philia—serves as a check against the destructive potential in eros. Celebrating agape—embracing love's spiritual source and significance—frees us to spread the life-giving energy of eros through our communities. Philia places love at the center of our everyday lives; agape brings us back to its deepest source. Let's be clear: eros and philia—our human, embodied loves—are not in conflict with agape. They depend upon it. Our deepest connections with friends, lovers, and family occur when we understand those relationships as part of a love that was working in the world long before any of us was born and will go on long after we're dead.

It's important not to confuse eros with libido. The two forces are related, but they're fundamentally different. Libido itself is a natural drive; without it the human race, and most of our fellow creatures, would have died out long ago. But if we engage with the object of our desire not as a person, but as a means to our own pleasure, libido degenerates into lust. That's why it's so important to distinguish between the reality of full, balanced eros—in which libido usually plays a part—and its grasping, warped shadows. When we equate eros with sex, we lose sight of its potential as creative love that draws energy from the spark of attraction between two people, and revels in the sensual joy of this messy, heart-breaking, beautiful world. Eros *can* be expressed in a sexual relationship, of course, but it can also bloom in collaborative art, athletic teamwork, and the ecstatic moments of worship that unite the faithful with one another and with God.

The conversations that led to this book began when Craig read Octavio Paz's *The Double Flame: Love and Eroticism*. Mesmerized by Paz's eclectic approach to spiritual sexuality, but sensing that something was missing, Craig asked Rhonda where he could learn more about Christianity and eros. When she recommended that he read the Christian poets, we discovered that we shared a love for Dante and John Donne. Our conversations led us to numerous other artists, musicians and writers, including James Baldwin and C.S. Lewis, whose classic study *The Four Loves*—he adds *storge*, the affection we share with children and animals, to the list—helped shape our conceptual framework.

From the beginning, our differing experiences enriched our conversations. Rhonda shares a Christian identity and orientation—if not every detail of theology—with the artists whose stories will guide us through this book. She's an Episcopal priest, who can make sense of her own life, and the workings of the universe, only in light of the life, death, and resurrection of Jesus Christ, and who can only live out that faith within the church. She knows that, because like Green she started down other paths before finally giving in to Jesus' persistent call in her thirties. Now the gospel is a source of hope, a guide to action, and a place to return to when she falls short of the call to love God and neighbor fully. To borrow a phrase from the book of the prophet Amos, the gospel is the "plumb line" calling her to continued conversion, spurring her to live her faith through action, and warning of the damage to herself and others when she ignores the call to love fully and honestly. Scripture and church tradition don't provide immediate answers to all her questions, but they always serve as the framework in which to ask them. The communion of saints—both ancestors and companions in this life—provides a community in which to discern God's call and answer it together.

Rhonda's story is inseparable from that community's story, and from daily life in the urban churches she has served. Life with the church members who try to live faithfully and know they need each other's support and challenge to do so. With visitors who arrive seeking something, but not necessarily knowing what it is—and often being surprised by that something when it finds them. And with the poor and homeless people who knock on the church doors or gather on its grounds, daring to hope the church will stand with them, and calling the church back to agape when we forget that it's both the source of our being and the power of Being itself.

Reverend Green, a brother in faith and a fellow pastor of the flock, knows all about building community with whomever God sends your way, and giving thanks for the gift each one brings. Sometimes that gift is hard to accept: when it points out your own flaws, teaches you patience the hard way, or shows you that eros is indeed a gift, but one that has to be enjoyed in faithful ways. For Rhonda, the church is the place where we practice loving everyone as God does, and where we particularly love those in need, trouble or despair, because the Bible teaches us that God loves them most of all. If the church isn't the place where we learn that love, it's not really the church.

In part because he grew up in and around churches oriented more toward fear than love, where eros was repressed and condemned, Craig's response is less clearly centered. Acutely aware of the way ideals are betrayed by the institutions that adapt them, he internalized a deep suspicion of organized religion and pledged never to pretend he'd experienced anything he wasn't sure he had. At the same time, he felt an abiding spiritual call. At different times, that call led him to explore the history of Christianity, Taoism, Jungian dream work, the writings of James Baldwin, Andre Comte-Sponville's *LittleBook of Atheist Spirituality*, and the West African religions that came together with Christianity at the center of the music that spoke to his deepest longings.

Not surprisingly, given his vocational path, the event that convinced him to return to a serious engagement with the church centered on music. In the summer of 2001, he was part of the teaching team for a course that took a group of students from the University of Wisconsin on a two-week bus tour of sites associated with the civil rights movement. One of the last stops was Memphis, where the group attended services at Al Green's church. There, wrapped in gospel music and the words of Scripture, supported by interlocking networks of philia, he felt something move in his soul, and heard a call that has continued to echo and direct his journey. Over the last decade, he's opened himself to the voice of the Holy Spirit (always aware that his understanding of that force would render him heretical in most Christian churches); attended Quaker services; fallen in love with Thomas Merton and the Gospel of Luke; contemplated the "desert fathers and mothers" of the third and fourth centuries who sought to disentangle Christianity from a corrupt power structure constituted in Jesus' name; and pondered whether that's possible today. *Love and Happiness* is part of his restless quest. What Craig and Rhonda share is that we're doing our best to hear, to live in response to, and to pass on, the call to manifest the power of love in our lives.

When we broached the idea for *Love and Happiness* to our friends, students, colleagues and parishioners, it became clear that we weren't the only ones thinking about these issues. At parties, in church gatherings, and after campus presentations, people were eager to share stories of their own (often about an unnamed "friend"). Everyone we met thirsted for an alternative to the trivialized love stories that dominate our pop culture. Too often, television, movies, self-help talk shows and popular music reduce the range of responses to eros to a choice between indulgence and repression. Advertising bombards us with images of sex as a consumer good, people as commodities whose sole purpose is to fulfill our immediate desires. The alternative many churches offer is no better, treating our sexuality as a currency to be exchanged for God's favor, a commodity in a spiritual marketplace.

The love stories we hear every day leave us suspended between a poorly conceived notion of desire and a poorly achieved notion of obedience. We hesitate to share our own stories for a host of reasons: we don't want to hurt those close to us; we worry about shocking, or boring, our friends; we're terrified of taking risks, or of sinking into moral chaos. Internal choruses of fear, guilt and shame silence us before we can get a word out. We're afraid those voices are right, feel ourselves unworthy of love. Not knowing who, if anyone, to trust with our stories, we bury them deep inside. Fearing that our friends won't understand our hopes and desires—or will tell us truths we don't want to hear—we cut ourselves off from philia. Expecting condemnation should we confess our dreams to the church, we lose faith in agape. But when we lock our erotic energy up in our heads, it magnifies the danger that eros will warp into lust.

People who want something more meaningful than the choice between indulgence and repression need to know they're not alone. They need, and want, better stories.

Dante, Shakespeare, Jane Austen and Al Green tell those stories. The core of *Love and Happiness* is what they tell us about the interconnections between eros, philia, and agape. Wrestling with the problem of eros in their own lives, these artists turned their experience into enduring works of art. Some of the stories they tell are horrifying, showing the devastation that warped love can wreak. Some are inspiring, helping us imagine the gift love can be in the here and now. Together, they offer us a vision of eros that's complex, sobering and ultimately deeply comforting.

As we explore the intricacies and practical applications of that vision, we'll follow the map of the erotic cosmos laid out in the Divine Comedy. Our first chapter, "'Love Is the Seed,' or, Dante's Garden of Demons and

Delight," follows Dante on his pilgrimage. Guided in turn by the classical poet Virgil, his own lost beloved Beatrice, and the Christian mystic Bernard of Clairvaux, Dante holds a mirror up to our common fallibility in the Inferno; learns how to bring the three loves into balance in the Purgatorio; and provides glimpses of true peace and harmony in the Paradiso. Each subsequent chapter turns to one of our title characters as a new, wise guide to part of that cosmos: Shakespeare to Hell, Jane Austen to Purgatory, Al Green to Heaven. Chapter Two, "Shakespeare's Blues, or, 'How Did I End Up in Hell, and Why Is It So Hard To Get Out?'" plunges us into demon-haunted worlds where social conventions and self-deception can warp eros into a destructive force. Chapter Three, "Jane Austen's Guide to the Feminist Purgatory, or, 'He (or sometimes She) Seemed Just Fine Until....'" turns to the practical problems of living with, and loving, each other in a world where erotic fantasy runs up against the harsh realities of repression and commodification. The final chapter, "'It's You I Want, but It's Him that I Need,' or, Imagining Paradise with the Reverend Al Green," lays out the possibilities for love and happiness, not in some distant future or escapist fantasy, but in human relationships that offer visions of Paradise in the here and now.

The conversations that led to *Love and Happiness* started in dialogue with the Christian tradition, and we use that vocabulary throughout the book. Although we believe our insights will be of value to people of any, or no, religious faith, we chose Christian terms for several reasons. First, it's personal, a reflection of our lived experience and the spiritual paths we've followed, not always within the church but always in conversation with it. The Christian terms we employ have somewhat different meanings for each of us, but we seek to use them with integrity, neither denying our convictions nor expecting the other to see things exactly as we do.

The second reason for our choice of the vocabulary involves context: it's an honest response to the artists we work with, all of whom were professed Christians. Dante and Al Green place Christianity at the center of their visions, while Shakespeare and Jane Austen were both deeply ambivalent toward the dominant forms of Christianity in their cultures. Our context matters too: for better or for worse, the Christian vocabulary is present in almost all public discussions in the United States. Using those terms allows us to participate in those discussions, while suggesting more fruitful directions they could take. We're suspicious both of the snap judgments of the religious right, and of liberal approaches that smooth honest disagreements into mush. Some Christians won't be comfortable with the breadth of our approach, and some non-Christians may get stuck on the religious language, but we think our readers are capable of engaging in dialogue and debate with the authors whose stories we're telling, with us, and with each other.

Finally, we've chosen the Christian vocabulary because Christianity is the faith that proclaims that God is love. You can look it up: 1 John 4:16 in the New Testament. The Greek word used for "love" in the passage is agape; historically, Christianity has had a complicated relationship with eros, desire, and sex. But that complicated relationship is often over-simplified: many Christians narrow the range of appropriate expressions of eros to exclude relationships that can be life-giving; and non-Christians (or disaffected former Christians) think the institutional church is more interested in damnation and repression than in love in any form. When the discussion is framed that way, as a choice between indulgence and repression, it's not surprising that fresh insights are rare.

Shaped by the Christian tradition, *Love and Happiness* reclaims a broader vision of love than many imagine is possible, proclaiming that eros, nurtured by philia, can lead us to agape. Eros draws its power from the longing to connect with another person and share our deepest selves, our minds, souls, and—often but not necessarily—bodies. Throughout the history of the Church, Christians who value eros have seen that desire as a reflection of God's longing to connect with us, and as a promise of the unity that we will one day experience with God and each other.

As Dante knew, the face of our beloved can draw us toward the face of God.

DAnTe

Chapter One

"'Love Is the Seed,' or, Dante's Garden of Demons and Delight"

Everyone who's read Dante's *Divine Comedy* has a story about how they first encountered it. For Craig the moment came at the fringes of conscious memory when he was seven years old. The son of a college teacher, he'd been taken to a faculty party where, bored with the conversation, he wandered off to the bookshelves. Who knows what caught his eye—maybe the woodcut of the man in strange clothes on the cover of the blue-bordered paperback, maybe the name of the translator, Henry Wadsworth Longfellow, the same as his elementary school's. Whatever the reason, he tucked himself away in a corner and spent the rest of the evening poring over the strange pictures and even stranger words. When it was time to go home, the big people found him asleep with his head on the book, which has been his companion ever since.

Rhonda was close to forty when Dante called her name. The moment arrived in a theology seminar devoted to the *Comedy*, when the professor, John Dally, described a scene from Susan Potter's play *Out to Lunch*. Two women go into a restaurant and sit down. Their waiter arrives and asks them, "What do you want?" When they start to ask about the specials of the day, he interrupts them, "No. What do you *want*?" Slowly, it dawns on them that the waiter is offering them *anything* they want; anything at all. Name it, and he'll deliver.

When John finished sketching the scene, he asked the class: "So: who was the waiter?"

Rhonda's immediate thought, spoken out loud, was: "He has to be the devil." A glance around the room confirmed she wasn't the only one who thought so. Everyone knew the story of Faust and its modern variations. Whatever our heart's desire, the devil can deliver. But there's always a really big catch: in exchange for giving us what we want, Satan holds the mortgage on our soul. Sooner or later he'll collect. The moral of the stories couldn't have been clearer: following our desires will land us in Hell.

But that *wasn't* the moral of the play. John, a student of literature who was intimately familiar with Marlowe, Goethe, and Thomas Mann, anticipated his students' suspicions, and chose the passage because it flipped the expected script. The waiter isn't the devil. He's God, and he's asking the characters in the play, and all of us, to think deeply on the question that can change our lives: "What do you *really* want?"

That's the question at the center of Dante's *Divine Comedy*. For the fourteenth-century Italian poet, as for most of us in the twenty-first century, the answer was "love." But as Dante well knew, that simple answer unleashes a seemingly infinite series of new questions: Whom, or what, do you *really* love? A person? Money? An image of yourself? How do you tell the difference between true love and simple lust? How can you be sure you're not just playing out a fantasy you saw in a movie or read in a book? Do you want to give love, or only to receive? Could you recognize true love if it found you, or is your heart too scarred by all the times you've been hurt? Do you want to possess your lover, or to live freely together? What happens if the one you love is married to someone else? How far will you go to get what you want? Would you flatter, lie, deceive? What if your church condemns your love? Who can you turn to for guidance when you've lost your way, and the face looking back from the mirror is the last one you'd trust? Is love an escape from the troubles of the world, or a sword and a shield to take back into the fray? Is love lifting you to Heaven or dragging you down to Hell?

Those questions, the ones that keep us awake at night, are where the *Divine Comedy* begins. When we meet Dante, he's wandering in a dark wood, alone, lost, overwhelmed by grief. The only woman he's ever loved, Beatrice, is dead. He's a political refugee fleeing from one Italian city to another. Cut off from community, feeling no compassion for himself or anyone else, his mind is an echo chamber reverberating with doubt and despair. Church, state, his beloved poetry: none of the things he's relied on shows him a way forward. His body and his soul are in danger. He's given up on love.

A lot of us know what that's like.

The book Dante called simply the *Comedy*—the *Divine* was bestowed by adoring readers—tells the story of the poet's recovery, his slow realization that love *is* the answer to his questions, not just a source of confusion. Or perhaps it would be more accurate to say the poem itself *is* his recovery, his discovery of what it means to truly love. The path it charts is still available to us, but it's not an easy one to find or to follow. We live in a culture that separates love from friendship, body from soul, heart from mind. We're constantly told that eros lives in the darkened bedroom, agape in church. They're opposites; we can have one or the other, but not both. As we'll show in this chapter, Dante tells us that's a false choice, that true eros and agape are absolutely inseparable. Nurtured by philia, the seeming opposites become part of a reality far more complex and creative than the televangelists and sex peddlers can even dream of.

Although the *Comedy* points the way to the world where the loves live in harmony, it began in erotic fantasy. Dante wrote his masterpiece for a woman he may have set eyes on only twice in his life: first when they were children of nine, and for the last time when they were 18. Beatrice and Dante were never alone together; they never touched; they never even talked to one another. Each entered into an arranged marriage, as their families expected. But for Dante none of that mattered. He thought of Beatrice obsessively, imagined impossible futures, and kept her at the center of his creative work. It may sound like a cliché, but from the moment he saw her, there was no other woman in the world for him.

Beatrice's death from the plague in 1290, at age 23, was one of two events that changed Dante's life forever. The other came twelve years later when he was forced into exile from Florence, a casualty of having backed the wrong party in the intricate politics of Italian city-states. Facing a sentence of death by fire should he return home, he stayed away the rest of his life. Devastated by his beloved's death, disillusioned by political failures, and separated from his family for years at a time, Dante devoted his life in exile to writing his masterpiece, finishing it just before his death from fever in 1321.

The plot of the *Divine Comedy* is simple: over the three days between Holy Thursday night and Easter Sunday morning 1300, Dante journeys through Hell, Purgatory and Paradise. Along the way, he meets a multitude of souls whose failings mirror his deepest fears about himself, and he learns the hard lessons of repentance and recovery. Besides Dante, the most important characters are his three guides: the Roman poet Virgil leads him through Hell and Purgatory; Beatrice into Paradise; and finally the monk-poet St. Bernard of Clairvaux, into God's dazzling presence. In our reading, each guide represents one of the three loves described in our introduction: Beatrice, eros; Virgil, philia; and Bernard, agape. Together, they help Dante confront his own flaws and mistakes, and teach him the real meaning and purpose of eros.

Dante knew from painful experience that eros can be a source of pain and confusion, but over the course of his voyage he learns that it's not an inherently destructive force. Eros isn't lust, a sin to be purged like gluttony or avarice. It's an intense love that can free our creative energies, deepen our connections with those around us, and set us on a path leading to the source of all life. If not for his erotic love for Beatrice, Dante would never have enjoyed his friendship with Virgil, or found the strength to undergo the disciplines of Purgatory. He might never have seen God.

Dante's worldview and vocabulary are deeply Christian, but you don't need to share that faith to walk the path beside him. In this chapter, we offer a new reading of his journey, one that honors the spiritual core of his art while making it accessible to people of all faiths, or none. Our approach leads to a clear but challenging conclusion: Eros has the potential to be a powerful creative force when it's lived within networks of philia, and suffused with agape. But that potential can only be realized if we heed a sobering corollary: abandoned to its own devices, eros can warp into lust and become one of the most destructive powers on the planet. Aware of both possibilities, the *Comedy* issues both a warning and an invitation, asking us to reflect on where we've lost our way, and calling us to imagine better paths. Read this way, Dante's poem becomes a guide to the always-perplexing puzzle of how to live love in our own day.

Dante for Moderns

Even people who haven't read a word of Dante know exactly what you mean when you say "there ought to be a special circle in Hell for. . . ." Same goes for the phrase carved above the gate to the Inferno: "Abandon all hope, ye who enter." Following in the footsteps of Michelangelo, Rosetti, Hieronymus Bosch, and Salvador Dalí, late twentieth and twenty-first century *dantistas* invoke the *Inferno* to describe suburbs, inner cities and the workings of the economic system. References to Dante's Hell abound in video games, television series, and heavy metal lyrics; journalists routinely assign villainous politicians and scandal-plagued celebrities to their proper niche among the damned. Today's fascination with the *Inferno* is nothing new; seven centuries of Dante's readers have focused on the first book of the *Comedy*, sometimes without bothering to read any further. Maybe the *Inferno* resonates so deeply with readers because every generation feels like it's living in the worst of times, and there's never a lack of evidence to support the theory. But if we remain content to watch the horror show of Hell, we're short-changing ourselves by more than two-thirds of what Dante's artistry offers us: we're throwing away a compass that could guide us out of the infernal abyss. The *Comedy* is a *comedy* because it's a story that ends happily, and to reach that happy ending we have to pay equal attention to all three parts.

Yet, next to the multiple, vividly imagined depictions of Hell, modern images of Purgatory and Paradise seem bland and simplistic. It's not that we're not interested in the subject matter of the last two books. Contemporary pop culture is obsessed with the practical concerns at the center of the *Purgatorio* and *Paradiso*: gaining self-awareness and imagining better ways to live. It's next to impossible to turn on cable TV or browse the front tables of chain bookstores without encountering earnest advice on how to get your life together. We *want* to find meaning in the wasteland or, failing that, simply to feel better about who and where we are.

A quick look at modern responses to Dante gives us some clues about why we have so much trouble realizing these desires. Different aspects of the problem surface when we look at the *Inferno*, the *Purgatorio*, and the *Paradiso*. Contemporary cartographers of Hell typically present damnation as a permanent condition. Fixated on the existential experience of torment, we stand motionless, contemplating the desolate landscapes of modern life. Trapped in loveless marriages, cogs in a (racist, sexist, capitalist, colonialist) machine, our condition is fixed, our fate sealed. The best we can do is analyze our situation with some measure of wit or ironic distance.

Such commentaries, however clever they may be, miss Dante's point. The suburbs or the ghettos may feel like Hell, but they aren't. We may feel dead, but we're not. The *Inferno* is a summons to action, not a spectacle to contemplate with refined revulsion. Dante calls on us not to analyze our damnation, but to change our lives, to own up to our desires and decide, together, what we're going to do about the mess we're in.

Making those changes requires moving through the *Comedy*. Dante understood creative and destructive desires, and he devoted the *Purgatorio* to thinking them through. Some of what he says parallels twenty-first century self-help wisdom. Accountability is a good thing; forgiving ourselves and others, a necessity. Twelve-step programs echo his belief that progress is impossible without the help of a "higher power." But even though his insights speak directly to the self-help industry's concerns, his worldview runs sharply against the modern grain. The problem lies in the label *self*-help: we want to believe we can pull ourselves out of the mire, and Dante knew that's just not possible. For him, any lasting, valuable change is a matter of love. We should love ourselves, of course, but love is an inherently communal enterprise. Without a vision of love that transcends the individual and unites us for a common creative purpose, the systems that promise to transform our suffering dissolve into simplistic, even narcissistic platitudes. The *Purgatorio* offers an antidote: a vision of healing and recovery as a shared process grounded in the three loves.

If contemporary versions of Purgatory devolve into self-help daydreams, our ideas about Paradise are usually little more than alabaster clichés. Pearly gates, choirs of angels under the direction of a conductor with a serious allergy to drums and guitars, and a bearded gatekeeper checking names against a vaguely theological version of Santa's list of the naughty and nice. Just as bad are the fundamentalist visions of Heaven as a prize reserved for the righteous, which will be all the sweeter because it's denied to so many.

Dante offers us an alternative to the saccharine-and-brimstone Heavens. The souls in the *Paradiso* are real people. They know their flaws and those of others, but they know those flaws don't define them. Repentant and thankful, they've taken their place in a world most of us can't begin to imagine: a place without hierarchy, where love is literally all that matters. Dante assures us that, if we're willing to take an honest—but not hopeless—look at Hell, and then do the hard work of Purgatory, the joy of Paradise can shape the rest of our lives.

A Brief Digression: Dante among the Paparazzi

And now a pause for the benefit of first-time (and many experienced) readers of the *Divine Comedy* who find themselves disoriented by Dante's seemingly arcane references to Italian politics and culture. For fourteenth-century readers, most of the souls occupying the circles of Hell were easily-recognizable celebrities, the subjects of the gossip that filled the Florentine equivalents of coffee shops and supermarket checkout lanes. If you squint just a bit, you can see the *Comedy* as a *People* magazine "Where are they now?" issue, satisfying our voyeuristic curiosity about how the major and minor celebrities of the moment finally turned out. To stretch the modern analogy a bit further, the *Comedy* also tapped into the appeal of PBS specials designed to make "highbrow" materials available to a wider audience. Dante's versions of Aristotelian philosophy and medieval cosmology possessed the appeal of documentaries on string theory, global warming, or the Supreme Court. Readers with the time, inclination, and a copiously foot-noted edition can eventually develop a detailed sense of the fourteenth-century "Who's Who," but the secret to enjoying a first reading of the *Comedy* is to relax and not worry about the minutiae.

Dante and Sin

For many contemporary readers, the *Comedy*'s treatment of sin is a bigger stumbling block than not knowing the specifics about the various sinners and saints. Although Dante consistently tries to be merciful in his judgments, he was working within the fourteenth-century's moral codes, which seem rigid and harsh to many in our own day. Some of the things that were then considered mortal sins—homosexuality and suicide, for instance—have been rethought by both church and state, and we no longer have a shared understanding of what "sin" means. When you mention the word, the first thing that comes to mind is likely to be the list of the "seven deadly sins" codified by Pope Gregory the Great in the sixth century: lust, wrath, envy, greed, gluttony, sloth, and pride. In 2008, the Vatican advanced a complementary list of the "seven social sins": "bioethical" sins, "morally dubious" experiments, drug abuse, polluting the environment, contributing to the widening divide between rich and poor, excessive wealth, and creating poverty. As with the sins of Dante's era, the specifics are open to debate. Is pride a destructive force for people who have been told their lives don't count? Are birth control and stem cell research liberating gifts, or hubristic tinkering with the natural order?

Catalogues of sins, as Dante was aware, are important not because they provide a checklist of behaviors to be avoided, but as starting points for thinking about the actions and attitudes that disrupt community and our connection to the highest values, whether or not we conceive of that as God. When we harden our hearts to suffering, indulge our desires without regard to the cost to others, break faith or betray our vows, we damage the connections that make it possible for eros to have a constructive presence in the world. The specific eros-related acts that cast souls into Purgatory or Hell are the same for us as they were for Dante: adultery, seduction, physical and emotional battering. When we treat each other as objects, surrender to jealousy and envy, or just forget to pay attention and give in to erotic sloth, we harm ourselves as well as others. Eros itself isn't a sin, but the powerful emotional and physical responses it triggers can overwhelm us and hurtle us toward Hell.

That's not to say that eros is an external force against which we are powerless. We can't evade responsibility by claiming that "the Devil made me do it." In the *Comedy*, the Devil has no power of his own, no say whatsoever in our ultimate fate. Nor does God condemn souls as a way of demonstrating his power over Satan and sin. "It's not a poem about 'you did this, you get this,'" poet Robert Pinsky observed. "It's about the mystery of how you hurt yourself. It's like the Talmud says: the evils others do to me are as nothing compared to the evils I do to myself." No one is *sent* anywhere in Dante's cosmos, the victim of a stern or capricious deity. Human beings are absolutely free, and God is absolutely just, and *will* give us what we truly desire. That's as much a warning as a promise, graphically illustrated both by the misery of Inferno's inhabitants and by the joy that permeates Paradise. The characters in the *Divine Comedy* end up where they do because of one thing, and one thing only: what they most love. Their experience after death reveals the truth—often hidden—about the lives they led.

Dante's vision is rooted in the theology of St. Augustine, the fourth century bishop usually remembered as a puritanical killjoy responsible for linking the doctrine of original sin with sex. That image distorts both Augustine's life and his attitude toward eros. As a young man, Augustine indulged his sensual desires and fathered a son with a woman who was the equivalent of his common-law wife; as he felt the pull of conversion to Christianity, he prayed, "make me chaste but not yet." His autobiography, *The Confessions*, is the story of how Augustine, intensely aware of the power of sexual desire and feeling his soul in danger, redirected his desire toward agape, reaching out to God in unabashedly erotic language: "You called, shouted, broke through my deafness; you flared, blazed, banished my blindness; you lavished your fragrance, I gasped, and now I pant for you; I tasted you, and I hunger and thirst; you touched me, and I burned for your peace."

For Augustine, love is a weight that pulls us toward our heart's desire, whatever that may be. To use his images: the connection we long for has the potential to draw us upward like a flame whose steady glow offers light and warmth, or drag us down like a stone in water, never to surface again. More often than not, eros is that flame, or that stone. For Dante, that flame blazed in the form of Beatrice.

Dante and Beatrice I

While the *Comedy* is the poem that immortalized Beatrice, it wasn't the only book Dante dedicated to her. The first, *La Vita Nuova*, devotes seventy-five pages of verses to extolling the splendors of erotic love. "New Life" was the crowning achievement of the *dolce stil nuovo*, the "new sweet style," a term Dante coined himself. It's not a stretch to think of him as medieval Florence's version of Smokey Robinson or Paul McCartney, crafting gorgeous lyrics that weave together celebrations of his beloved's charms with obsessive reports on the state of his emotional weather. Even the smallest gesture—a passing glance, a flutter in her voice—could unleash storms of passion, remorse, or despair. *You really got a hold on me. Yesterday all my troubles seemed so far away.*

A beautifully polished, deeply felt masterpiece, *La Vita Nuova* was the fulfillment of every young poet's dream, a suite of verses so smooth, so seductive, they'd be impossible to resist. The poem circles around a single theme: Dante wants Beatrice to smile at him, to meet his eyes and acknowledge his presence, a simple blessing that would be "the end of all my desires." The sole purpose of his life and poetry is to praise Beatrice; writing about anything or anyone else would be an infidelity. His beloved is an angel missing from Heaven, and he shivers at the sight of her, sure that "every saint cries out for this grace." Her power is such that "what she gives him"—even the merest glance—"turns into salvation." The fate of his (erotically obsessed) soul is in her hands.

When Dante began writing *La Vita Nuova*, Beatrice was still alive and that image was part of a poetic game, a rhetorical move akin to the plaintive, "If you leave me, I'll die." Seven years after he wrote the first of the poems included in the book, Beatrice was actually dead. The game had come to an end, leaving Dante languishing in the emotional Hell reserved for frustrated lovers. Feeling a grief that's much more than rhetorical, he admits that he misunderstood Beatrice's role in his life and resolves "to write no more of this blessed one until I [can] more worthily treat of her." Still working within the conventions of the *dolce stil nuovo*, he declares that he wants to die, so that his soul can do what his body can't, and "go to see the glory" of his beloved in Paradise. But first, he promises, he will write another book, the likes of which had never been written about any woman.

Dante in Hell

The *Divine Comedy* fulfills that vow. Determined not to romanticize or trivialize his love for Beatrice, Dante charts a path that begins at a point of total despair. The opening stanza of the *Inferno* presents Dante alone in a "dark" or "shadowed" wood, the "right road" or "straight way" "blurred" or "lost." However you translate the key lines—"*mi ritrovai per una selva oscura, che la diritta via era smarrita*"—, the speaker is confused and disoriented. He's lost, and he doesn't have the emotional strength or moral clarity to move ahead. In contemporary terms, he's depressed, in a spiritual crisis, one of the joyless souls mechanically going through the daily motions with no real sense of purpose. He's given up on love in all its forms.

Before launching his protagonist on his journey, Dante makes a crucial poetic move, establishing a distance between the self who's experiencing the poem's events—the pilgrim about to enter the Inferno—and the poet looking back on the pilgrim's voyage. The distinction between Dante the pilgrim and Dante the poet is crucial to the *Comedy*'s picture of the psychology of healing. "Ah, it is hard to speak of what it was, that savage forest," Dante the poet writes with a survivor's shudder. Looking back after the end of the journey, he testifies to the necessity of telling the hard truth, the whole story. "But to retell the good discovered there . . . I'll also tell the other things I saw." Early in the first canto, Dante the poet makes it clear that Dante the pilgrim can't make the journey alone. As he wanders in the dark wood, he looks up and sees the light "which serves to lead men straight along all roads" bathing the peaks high above. Summoning his resolve, he rests for a moment, then sets out, only to find his path blocked by a leopard, a symbol of lust, which "so impeded my ascent that I had often to turn back again." The fact that Dante's sexual desire is separated from the other loves is at the root of his spiritual struggle.

Unexpectedly—and, Dante makes clear, through no act of his own—he receives help from three women who embody the loving connection he's lost: Beatrice (eros), St. Lucy (philia), and the Virgin Mary (agape) who, as embodiments of divine love, sets the rescue in motion. As Beatrice enjoys a quiet conversation with the biblical matriarch Rachel, Mary looks down at Earth and notices the poet's distress. She dispatches Lucy, patron saint of vision, to remind Beatrice of her unbroken connection to Dante: "Your faithful one needs you now . . . Don't you hear his pitiful weeping?" Beatrice recognizes that the grief-stricken Dante isn't yet ready to handle her presence, so she summons Virgil, traditionally seen as the symbol of reason, and in our reading the embodiment of philia. She calls on him to help "my friend, who is no friend of fortune" and assures him of her good motives: "Love moved me and makes me speak."

Virgil readily accepts his commission, freeing Beatrice to return to Paradise, but Dante, mired in hopelessness, is harder to convince. When Virgil urges him to undertake the voyage through the next world, he pleads exhaustion. He's a mere mortal, a failure no one in their right mind should bother with. "Neither I nor any man thinks me fit for this," he protests. "If I commit myself to go I fear lest my going be folly." Goading Dante for his failure as a *man*, Virgil calls him a coward and reminds him sharply that, however abused he feels, he has in fact received a priceless gift: "Why art thou not bold and free, when three such blessed ladies care for thee in the court of Heaven and my words promise thee so much good?" Moved by the proof of Beatrice's love and the promise of Virgil's friendship, Dante agrees to undertake this strange journey. Immediately, however, he quails before the now-famous inscription: "Abandon all hope, ye that enter." Sympathetic but firm, Virgil takes his hand, and together they pass through the gate of Hell.

The physical and psychological punishments Dante and Virgil witness as they descend through the nine circles of Hell fit the sins with horrifying precision. The violent are immersed in rivers of boiling blood; heretics entombed in red-hot sepulchers; the gluttonous pelted by filthy rain. False prophets walk with their heads on backwards, hypocrites stagger beneath the weight of outwardly beautiful robes filled with lead, schismatics are torn apart by swords. In the lowest rings of the lowest circle, traitors are frozen in ice. Throughout, the damned and the demons who torment them are locked in gyrations of rage, recrimination and regret.

Visual recreations of Hell—Michelangelo's *The Last Judgment*, the "Hell" panel from Hieronymus Bosch's *Garden of Earthly Delights*, Salvador Dalí's woodcuts of the *Inferno*—typically assign starring roles to the demons. Cavorting gleefully, they radiate a malicious, inventive energy as they impale their victims or drag them down to the pit. For Dante, however, demons are minor characters, flunkies who snarl impotent invective as they carry out the boring tasks they've been assigned for eternity. The reason they play such a minor role is simple: the *Inferno* doesn't *need* compelling demons. The inmates of Hell carry their own demons with them, in the form of their unrepented sins. Dante's understanding of demons anticipates the twentieth century theologian Paul Tillich, who wrote "The claim of anything finite to be final in its own right is demonic." In other words, anything we value more than the ultimate—more than God, more than deep, balanced, life-giving love—*becomes* our demon, luring us to worship it and repaying our devotion by destroying us. Demons aren't pure evil, or they wouldn't have the power over us that they do. Rather, they entice us with something good and beautiful, something that could be holy and healing, but they warp it, and us. That's why Tillich described the condition of being demon-possessed as "the state of being split."

Dante's misery stems from his split desires, and early in the *Inferno* he meets his personal demon: eros distorted into lust. After passing through Limbo, the bland, pleasant-enough circle of Hell occupied by the "virtuous pagans" who lived good lives but never heard of Jesus Christ, Virgil and Dante enter the second circle, reserved for the lustful. There, those "who sinned within the flesh, subjecting reason to the rule of lust" are buffeted about by the winds of a "hellish hurricane, which never rests." Lust, as Dante knew well, offers no resting point, no peace. Listening to the moans and laments of the "guilty spirits," he writes, with a shudder, "There is no hope that ever comforts them—no hope for rest and none for lesser pain."

As he will do throughout the journey, Virgil identifies several of the most famous of the souls twisting and turning in the wind: the Assyrian queen Semiramis, who legalized all manner of licentious behavior, including incest, to indulge her own desires; Dido, who committed suicide in a fit of erotic despair over her unrequited love for Aeneas; Cleopatra, Helen of Troy and "more than a thousand shades departed from our life because of love." Virgil intends the stories as warnings, but Dante, still in despair over Beatrice, is overcome by sympathy: "pity seized me, and I was like a man astray." For a poet who spent the first part of his career writing praises of overpowering love, that pity is understandable, probably inevitable. But it's also fodder for Dante's demons, the parts of his psyche that whisper seductively that there's really nothing wrong with letting desire have the final word.

Dante's vacillations between self-knowledge and evasion come to a head when he encounters the lovers Paolo and Francesca, murdered by Francesca's husband—Paolo's brother—when he found them in an erotic embrace. Now they're doomed to spend eternity intertwined with each other. As Francesca tells the story, she focuses not on its violent denouement, but on the powerful, mutual eros that brought the lovers together. "Love, that can quickly seize the gentle heart, took hold of him because of the fair body [now] taken from me," she laments. "Love, that releases no beloved from loving, took hold of me so strongly through his beauty that, as you see, it has not left me yet." Hearing the language of love he had placed at the center of *La Vita Nuova* on Francesca's lips, Dante empathizes with the fate of the lovers joined for eternity. "Alas, how many gentle thoughts, how deep a longing, had led them to the agonizing pass!" While he stops short of questioning divine justice, Dante tells Francesca that her "afflictions move me to tears of sorrow and of pity" and begs her to tell him how eros acted on the lovers "in the time of gentle sighs."

Lamenting that "there is no greater sorrow than thinking back upon a happy time in misery," Francesca tells Dante of how a shared love of poetry led to the lovers' fall. As she and Paolo sat alone reading the Arthurian legend of the adulterous lovers Lancelot and Guinevere, they entered more and more deeply into the story. When they reached the description of "how the desired smile was kissed," they took on the roles themselves. "This one, who never shall be parted from me," Francesca says, transforming the stock romantic image into a reminder of her torment, "while all his body trembled, kissed my mouth . . . That day we read no more."

Both the general situation and the specific details carry disquieting echoes for a writer of erotically-charged lyrics in love with a married woman. Francesca assigns "the book and he who wrote it" the role of Gallehault, the go-between who encouraged Lancelot and Guinevere in their illicit love. Realizing that *La Vita Nuova* might, and doubtless had, contributed to similar scenarios, Dante is overcome with emotion. Unable or unwilling to take a long look in this particular mirror, he faints.

Countless readers over the centuries have found Paolo and Francesca's assignment to Hell unjust. At first glance, they would seem to belong with the souls walking through the fires on the seventh terrace of Purgatory where the lustful repent their sins of the flesh. Especially for modern readers living in a world where large numbers of people, including many Christians, accept divorce and recreational sex as matters of course, the punishment seems disproportionate. Readers resist the scene, in part, because of the lack of distance between the doomed lovers and Dante the pilgrim. He sympathizes with them deeply and personally, allowing his emotions to overwhelm him.

For Dante the poet, that's exactly the problem, and the point. In the moment, eros can be all-consuming, a demon masquerading as a god. As long as we remain in its literal, or even its figurative, embrace, we'll be unable to remember our broader ties of philia, or to heed the higher call of agape. Paolo and Francesca aren't damned because of their sexual connection in itself; as we'll see later, if they had repented of it they might have ended up in Purgatory. Instead, they failed to take responsibility for their actions, to acknowledge whom, and what, they had betrayed. As Dante listens to the story, memories of Beatrice stirring his emotions, he's very much involved. It will take him and his readers many more steps to understand, and accept, what the story of Paolo and Francesca really means.

As Dante the poet underscores, Dante the pilgrim must learn that lust isn't simply a momentary surrender of physical self-control. Instead, it's a force that motivates violence, fraud and treachery, the sins punished in the deepest circles of Hell. When Dante's descent brings him to the eighth circle, the *Malebolge* (or "evil pockets"), he encounters a multitude of naked sinners, some pursued by horned demons brandishing whips, others submerged in human excrement. Under Virgil's watchful eye, he talks to a man who pimped his sister to a nobleman in hope of personal gain; and he contemplates the Greek hero Jason who seduced and abandoned a series of women, among them Medea, who took revenge by murdering their children. The inhabitants of the ninth, and lowest, circle include Francesca's husband Gianciatto, who killed her and Paolo in his jealous rage. Condemned for betraying his kin, Gianciatto is immersed head-down in icy waste, in the company of Judas and Lucifer. The tour of the damned that began with lovers succumbing to the promised joys of the flesh ends with stark images of violence and betrayal. Separated from philia and agape, Dante learns, eros can lead us straight down to the nadir of the universe.

The souls Dante meets in the Inferno have, at best, only one faint hope: that the living will remember them with compassion. Although they know all too well why they were condemned, it's too late for them to do anything about it. Their only purpose now is to be a lesson to the rest of us.

The *Comedy* doesn't end in the depths of Hell. Dante emerges from the Inferno, looks up and, far above, sees the stars, a reminder that harmony, real love, *is* possible. His guides will help him as he moves toward the stars' beckoning light, learning the hard lessons of repentance and hope.

DANTE IN PURGATORY

The arrival of new souls in Purgatory couldn't be more different from the unloading of the condemned in the Inferno. The damned arrive cursing each other and Charon, the boatman who carried them over Acheron, the river of death. Their cacophonous cries fill the air; no music soothes their torment. In contrast, the souls arriving in Purgatory are singing "all together with one voice." The psalm that had been their funeral hymn, "When Israel came out of Egypt," turns into a gospel chorus praising the God "who turned the hard rock into a pool of water and flint-stone into a flowing spring." These pilgrim souls have no idea how long their journey will take—there's no standard exchange rate of years in Purgatory per sinful act—but they do know that, since they've entered Purgatory, they will one day arrive in Paradise.

As Dante walks through Purgatory's gates, the first thing he hears is the "Te Deum," the hymn sung at Matins, the first prayer service of the day in monastic communities. That hymn of praise is a perfect introduction to Purgatory. Purgatory was originally a twelfth century Catholic concept allowing for the souls of the repentant dead to be purified before entering into God's presence. Steeped in that tradition, Dante presents Purgatory as a *church*, a place where souls come together in the spirit of fellowship, sharing music and conversation, supporting one another in the shared task of spiritual growth. Like earthly churches, and any community seriously dedicated to spiritual and psychological healing, Purgatory is filled with half-formed understandings, justifications, longings, desires, struggles. Flawed and human, the pilgrim souls who crowd its steep terrain have more in common with Dante the sinner than with Beatrice the saint. Unlike the inmates of the Inferno—alone with their sins forever, unable to connect across their misery—they journey together to a better life, growing and changing as they go. Dante called the residents of Hell "the lost people"; those in Purgatory are "the new people," making a fresh and joyful start.

Their voyage isn't easy. Purgatory is an island mountain, made up of seven progressively higher terraces. The ascent is arduous, a sharp climb from terrace to terrace along narrow paths next to precipitous drops. Along the way, souls have to unlearn old habits and develop new, healthier ones. Anyone who has trained for an athletic event, changed their diet after a health scare, taken up meditation, or entered into a 12-step program has at least a faint idea of the challenges they face. Dante will experience those disciplines first-hand as he is purged of his besetting sins: pride, lust, and anger. In the Inferno, he was an observer; in Purgatory, he is a fellow pilgrim, sweating his way to Paradise with his brothers and sisters. The blessing of Purgatory is that philia abounds. Confident that all of them, without exception, are held within agape's embrace, the sojourners are free from jealousy and can struggle together, encouraging one another with music and prayer as they walk their common path.

Which is to say, Purgatory is a place of *repentance*. Repentance isn't simply a matter of feeling sorry for what one has done, asking forgiveness, and promising not to do it again. Repentance is nothing less than a fundamental change in desire. Dante understood that as a turning from sin towards God, but repentance isn't just a Christian concept, and it can resonate even with those who claim no religious faith. Anyone who's ever screwed up, felt ashamed, and stood at the crossroads wondering which way to go, faces the same questions: How did I get here? How do I make amends? Can they ever forgive me? Can I forgive myself? Where can I go from here? What do I *do*?

Dante's answer to that final question offers a pathway out of confusion, for seekers inside and outside the church. The first steps are clear, if not easy: desire change, tell the truth, and, most importantly, open yourself to agape. Dante makes one clear, hopeful promise: as long as we're alive, it's never too late to start over, to accept compassionate love. On the outskirts of Purgatory, he encounters Buonconte da Monfeltro, his adversary in an important battle for Florence. Most of Dante's contemporaries would have assumed, as he did, that Buonconte had ended up in Hell. Buonconte's uncatalogued sins are so notorious that after he died in combat with no priest nearby to absolve him, not even his wife bothered to pray for his salvation. But in talking with this infamous man who had once been his enemy, Dante learns that Buonconte died making the sign of the cross over his chest and calling the name of the Virgin Mary. When God sends an angel to collect Buonconte's soul, Satan is outraged, but the Lord of Hell is powerless in the face of Buonconte's heartfelt desire for God. That last-minute longing is enough to pull the sinner up out of the abyss.

Both for those who like Buonconte were "sinners up to the last hour" and for those who have struggled to walk the path throughout their lives, Purgatory is a place of intense suffering; the medieval church declared that each instant of penitential pain was worse than the most intense pain a person could suffer in the material world. But it's also a place of love. Identifying love as the seed of virtue *and* of "all acts deserving punishment," Virgil enumerates three types of deformed love: perverted love (the proud, the envious, the wrathful), defective love (the slothful), and excessive love (the gluttonous, the greedy and the lustful.) Sinners in the first group love it when evil things happen to others; those in the second group feel only tepid desires and succumb to lassitude and distraction.

While Dante is attentive to all of the sinners, he is particularly interested in, and sympathetic to, the third group, especially the souls on the seventh terrace, who repent the sins of the flesh. Like Dante, the lustful love strongly, but have trouble directing their love in the right direction. "Serving [their] appetites like beasts," they spent their life in the pursuit of sex, reducing themselves and their quarry to objects. Aware of his friend's susceptibility to love stories, Virgil commands Dante to keep his eyes on the narrow path. Noting the flames that shoot from the mountain's steep walls, Dante admits honestly, "I feared the fire on this hand and on that feared to fall below." The lustful walk a circular path, heterosexuals moving to the right, homosexuals to the left. In the fourteenth century, there wasn't a concept of "straight" or "gay" as we use the terms now, but Dante's enduring insight applies to all sexual orientations and gender identities: we shouldn't treat lovers as disposable commodities. The souls circling the seventh terrace must learn to encounter one another not as bodies that can fulfill their desires, but as friends sharing a journey. When they encounter one another, they pause briefly, embrace in the spirit of philia and continue on, singing and praising the saints who maintained chastity in the face of temptation. The specific object of their lust isn't the root of these penitents' sin. Instead, they erred by failing to connect eros with the other loves.

Both of the souls Dante speaks to on the seventh terrace are poets: Guido Guinizelli, who Dante credited with founding the *dolce stil nuovo*, and the twelfth century Provençal troubadour Arnaut Daniel.

Like the French romancers whose words seduced Paolo and Francesca, Guinizzelli and Arnaut's poetry runs the constant risk of idolatry. The charms of the beloved can become so compelling that they seem the source of all meaning, all love. The excesses of feeling that course through the poetry of, to cite more familiar examples, John Donne, Walt Whitman or Emily Dickinson, can be a thing of real beauty, and Dante's treatment of Guinizzelli and Arnaut makes it clear that he identifies deeply with them. But if erotic desire remains *all*-encompassing, it can plunge lovers into Hell.

What distinguishes Guinizzeli and Arnaut from Paolo and Francesca is that the poets repented of their sins. Dante knows that true repentance is not a matter of paying lip service to what we're supposed to believe, appearing to live the way polite society expects us to. It's a much more serious and joyful thing. Repentance means turning away from the path we've been on, and starting to move in a different direction. That movement doesn't happen in a single moment; it's a process that takes time, and needs the company of others to flourish. That's why the flawed but hopeful souls in Purgatory continue to encourage each other on their journey. They're not renouncing eros, only its warped forms. After their purgation is finished, they'll be able to trust themselves and each other completely, and welcome the experience of eros in harmony with the other loves.

Knowing that repentance is necessary is one thing; carrying it out is another. Before Dante can realize his dream and gaze into Beatrice's eyes, he must pass through the fire and purge himself of lust. As a veteran of war and political persecutions, Dante recoils from the fire, remembering "bodies I once saw burned." Virgil attempts to reason with him, assuring him "there is no suffering here, no death." When Dante continues to resist, his mentor invokes the power of eros. "This wall," he reminds Dante, indicating the flames, "stands between you and Beatrice." Preceding Dante into the fire, Virgil urges his friend on with the promised fulfillment of his erotic dream, calling back, "I seem to see her eyes already." As Dante follows his guide and feels the purging fire burning away the lust within him, sacred music beckons them onward: "*Venite, benedicti Patris mei,*" "Come, you that are blessed by my Father," an anthem drawn from Matthew's Gospel which continues, "inherit the kingdom prepared for you from the foundation of the world." The music is an implicit reminder to Dante that what awaits him is not just eros, not just the woman he has dreamed of for years, but a deeper love and richer promise. Accompanied by philia, spurred on by eros, and beginning to gain a new understanding of agape, Dante emerges from the purifying flames.

What happens next is one of the most moving and devastating scenes in all of literature. As they reach the top step of Purgatory's highest terrace, Virgil leaves. Having guided Dante as far as he can "with understanding and with skill," Virgil can "discern no further." For Dante, the pagan poet represented reason, which can't imagine, let alone understand, the promise of Paradise. In our reading, Virgil embodies philia, the companion who pulled his brother out of the abyss of despair and got him started on the long voyage of recovery. Now it's time for another guide to take over, time for Dante to learn from Beatrice the true meaning and value of eros.

Virgil sends his friend on his way with a symbolic gift. Assuring Dante that his will is now truly "free, upright and whole," the ancient poet demonstrates his confidence by saying, "over yourself I crown and miter you." Dante has seen and heard the warnings of the Inferno; he has been purged of the impulses that divert his love and divide his will. When Virgil tells him "let your pleasure be your guide," he hears the words not as an invitation to hedonistic self-indulgence but as an affirmation that he can now make decisions guided, not by what is "correct," "sensible," or "acceptable," but by his deepest desires. For the first time, Dante can trust his own free will in all spheres of his life, because his deepest desire is to live out the vision of harmonious loves.

It's a testimony to the power of eros that the first thing Dante does when he meets Beatrice is forget what he's just learned.

Dante and Beatrice 2

Following the script of *La Vita Nuova*, Dante expects a joyful romantic reunion with Beatrice. What he gets is, in the words of Dante scholar Peter Hawkins, a "lover's quarrel." He's walked through fire for Beatrice and parted from his dearest friend forever. In return he receives, not a welcoming embrace, but a rebuke. Before he can walk alongside his beloved, Dante must take to heart what he has learned during his voyage through Hell and Purgatory: eros *is* a part of Heaven, but erotic love is *not* in itself Paradise. It's a lesson he, and everyone who feels the power of eros at its most extreme, has to learn and re-learn.

The first thing Beatrice does is to insist that Dante talk, without evasion, about the behavior that set him adrift in the dark wood. She doesn't just refuse her role in his erotic fantasy; she wants him to understand what was wrong with that fantasy in the first place, so he can apply the lesson when his pilgrimage ends. Agape and philia led her down to Hell to get him out of his mess, but he needs to understand that it wasn't so that they could live happily ever after, just the two of them. She's not a creature put on earth for his pleasure, but a being with her own spiritual destiny. She knows her words will wound Dante, and she also knows he needs to hear them; sometimes agape-filled eros has to speak in a stern voice. As tears stream down Dante's face, she begins ominously, "weep not yet, for you must weep for another sword." Taken aback by her rebuke, unwilling to admit the mistakes that brought him to the edge of the Inferno, Dante drops his eyes. Seeing his reflection in the stream that stands between him and Beatrice, he draws back, "so great shame weighed on my brow."

At first Dante hopes that this emotional recoil is all that will be required of him, but he soon learns that Beatrice has a higher, more difficult goal in mind than simply shaming him. The angels who surround Beatrice take pity and sing a psalm of repentance: "*In te, Domine, speravi...*" "In you, O Lord, have I taken refuge; let me never be put to shame." Hoping for quick forgiveness, Dante takes the psalm as a sign of absolution, but Beatrice stands firm. "Sin and sorrow," she reminds the heavenly choir, must "be of one measure." Agape promises forgiveness, but without unflinching honesty and real repentance, both the penitent and the one forgiving are simply acting out a charade. Beatrice isn't being legalistic, demanding a metaphorical eye for an eye, nor does she want Dante to wallow in self-castigation. He's not unique; scores of others have made the same mistakes before him. Beatrice is simply reminding him that if shame is to be a first step toward spiritual growth, it has to be followed by humility and honesty.

Reviewing the history of their relationship, Beatrice reminds Dante that when he was young, eros spurred him to do good. In her words, "Showing him my youthful eyes I brought him with me, bound on the right way." But when she died—from her perspective, "changed life"—he lost faith in love and "gave himself to another," not another woman, but the desire for political success and earthly fame. When that quest broke his heart, Dante succumbed to a loveless despair, allowing it to hold him in its grip until Beatrice traveled to Hell to start him on his journey of recovery. "For this," she notes sharply, "I visited the threshold of the dead." Now, faced with the woman who refused to abandon him, Dante must tell the truth about who he is, where he's been and what he's done. Only after he's taken responsibility for his actions will Beatrice allow him to leave them in the past.

Dante's confession is quick, heartfelt, and tearful: "Present things with their false pleasure turned my steps as soon as your face was hid." When she died, he veered off the creative, life-giving path that eros had shown him, and became embroiled in earthly politics governed by rational calculations of short-term interest. Once Dante has made that confession, he can drink from Lethe, the river of blessed forgetting that marks the boundary of Paradise, and continue his instruction in the varieties and purpose of love. The devastating, hopeless longing he bore for over ten years, to see Beatrice's face again, is finally satisfied, and Dante has a new understanding of his love's true purpose.

Dante's erotic love for Beatrice transcends physical desire. It's a gift from God, a glimpse of divine beauty, and he needs to complete his pilgrimage so he can share what he learns about love with the world. In return for Dante's repentance, Beatrice promises to stay with him as he journeys through Paradise. Having witnessed the consequences of sin and participated in the process of repentance, Dante has learned that, in their truest form, the three loves are inseparable. Eros leads us to agape and strengthens philia; agape suffuses philia and equips us to enjoy and express eros fully. Guided by the creative power that animates the ever-changing world, sexual love is not an end in itself, but an intrinsic part of a harmony we can only begin to imagine.

The lesson of Purgatory firmly in mind, his eyes once again on the stars above, his beloved beside him, Dante is ready to see Heaven.

The Vision of Paradise

For Dante, as for almost all modern readers, Paradise hovers on the edge of absolute incomprehensibility. Emanating a strange, elusive beauty, the images filling the final book of the *Divine Comedy* stretch the imagination, challenging us to think and feel beyond the limits of our everyday reality: lights within lights, wheels within wheels, inconceivably complex musical harmonies. For some readers, it's a breathtaking vision of harmony; for others, it seems abstract, a fuzzy dream divorced from the conditions of everyday life. Aware that we can't experience the vision directly, as Beatrice and the saints do, Dante doesn't give us a blueprint for building the heavenly city here on earth. Rather, he offers us a glimpse of what true love, and the peace it creates, might mean if we let ourselves be guided by our spiritual traditions, our elders (Dante among them), and the sisters and brothers who help us imagine a world where we live in harmony with ourselves and others, freed from the torments of unfulfilled desire.

The Paradise Dante shows us is filled with recognizable human beings, but one of the first lessons he learns in Heaven is the utter irrelevance of the hierarchies that the living create to distinguish between those who are, and aren't, "worthy" of love. Newly arrived from Purgatory, Beatrice at his side, Dante perceives Paradise as a series of ascending spheres, each of whose inhabitants sit progressively closer to God. Arriving at the "lowest sphere," the home of the saints who were guilty of breaking vows, Dante asks Piccarda, a sympathetic soul: "do you who are happy here desire a higher place, that you may see more and become more dear?" She gently reassures Dante that each soul in Paradise is happy where it has been placed. Their wills have become one with God's; in Paradise agape—often called "charity" in the world—is *necesse*, simple logical necessity, the way things are. "It was clear to me then," Dante reflects, "that everywhere in Heaven is Paradise."

There are no cheap seats in Heaven, no slave gallery, no pew from which women gaze at a pulpit they're deemed unworthy to enter. It's a true community, united by shared purpose and mutual love. The division of Paradise into concentric spheres drawing ever-closer to God's presence is simply an illusion for Dante's benefit. It's the only way his limited human understanding can grasp the degrees and types of spiritual perfection. Ranking the saints makes no more sense than blaming a peacock for not soaring like a hawk, or a drum for not playing melody like a flute. The saints know and accept themselves fully, and whatever their soul's capacity, it's filled to the brim with love for God, each other, and the world outside the heavenly spheres. Everyone matters, everyone has value, but we're not all the same. It's a liberating vision, one that lets us appreciate one another not only for who we are and what we do, but simply *because* we are. It's a vision of harmony consistent not only with Christianity, but with true democracy and any other set of values that believes in the inherent worth and dignity of every human being. We may never attain it in its perfect form, but if we let it be our compass, we're far less likely to fall into the behaviors that disrupt communities and betray our ideals.

Closer to peace than he has ever been, Dante moves through this realm of deep love side by side with "the lady who imparadises my mind." Beatrice responds gently to Dante's questions as he listens to scholars and saints contemplating questions of fate and free will; salvation, sin, and resurrection; unity and multiplicity; science as a path toward truth; the mystery of time in a sphere where "there was no *after*, no *before*." In the sphere of the sun, St. Thomas Aquinas and eleven other spirits of the wise form themselves into a crown around Dante and Beatrice. Together, they witness a dance of souls echoing the harmony of the astronomical spheres; and the formation of an eagle of light that radiates a vision of world government founded on principles of justice and the higher love. Awestruck by the peace and joy he feels in his beloved's presence, Dante reaches for images to express what he feels. He describes his state in musical terms as a plainsong wherein "a voice in voice is heard—one holds the note, the other comes and goes." Later, he imagines it as the beauty that fills the sky when "concentric, like in color, two rainbows curve their way through a thin cloud," "the outer rainbow echoing the inner." Experiencing his love for Beatrice more and more as a pathway to agape, he sees her smile is no longer as an end in itself, but as "a signal that made the wings of my desire grow." When Dante realizes this, he's very close to God.

That doesn't mean Dante has stopped being human. Standing beside Beatrice, having learned many of the lessons that Dante the poet will place at the center of the *Comedy*, Dante the pilgrim feels as if he has realized his soul's dream. But just as he had to part from Virgil, Dante must endure a second sundering when Beatrice returns to her place in Paradise, leaving him in the care of Saint Bernard of Clairvaux. As it was with Virgil, the parting comes as a stunningly unexpected shock. Taking in the vision of a new sphere of Paradise, Dante turns to ask Beatrice yet another question about what he's seeing. "I thought to see Beatrice," Dante writes, "and I saw an old man. . .His eyes and his cheeks were suffused with a gracious gladness," his whole manner "of such kindness as befits a tender father." Bernard tells Dante that his beloved has returned to the place among the saints that she left to come to his aid. She's completed the mission in which eros, agape, and philia all came together, and now it's time to entrust Dante to another guide so she can return to communion with God and her fellow saints.

As Dante searches for one last glimpse of his beloved, he remembers that in Paradise, distance is an illusion. Beatrice's place is immeasurably far from him in human terms, but "to me it made no difference, for her image came down to me undimmed." Beatrice smiles at him one last time, then turns her face back toward God. Death has once more separated her from Dante, but this time he knows that the love that unites them is something that death can't kill. He has the hope that he'll see Beatrice again, once his earthly life has ended, and now he understands the true gift their eros has given him. It has put him on the path that will eventually lead him back to that place of overflowing, eternal love, where together they will rejoice in the presence of God, each other, and the whole heavenly community.

St. Bernard and the Song of Songs

It's no accident that Dante's guide through the final cantos of the *Comedy* is Bernard de Clairvaux, a monk who wrote 86 sermons on the Bible's most exuberantly erotic book, the Song of Songs. Traditionally attributed to King Solomon, but now thought by many to have been written by a woman, the Song chronicles the erotic awakening of the Shulamite, a young woman reveling in the discovery of herself, her lover, and the eros that energizes the world around them. She celebrates the blurring of boundaries between her beloved, herself, and the rest of creation in lyrics like, "I am a rose of Sharon, a lily of the valleys.... As an apple tree among the trees of the wood, so is my beloved among young men. With great delight I sat in his shadow, and his fruit was sweet to my taste." Their union blends eros and philia in a way Dante is learning to understand: "His mouth is sweet wine, he is all delight. This is my beloved, and this is my friend, O daughters of Jerusalem." Bursting with vitality, the Shulamite pursues her love without shame and revels in their time together, despite their community's attempts to enforce "proper" boundaries.

That's not to say that agape is missing from the Song of Songs. Although the poem never mentions God by name, the vast majority of Jewish and Christian commentators have read it as an allegory about the divine love for humanity. They've also seen a microcosm of that rich love in the earthly union of two people—a view that makes the Song a popular choice for wedding readings. Bernard stood in that tradition: fully understanding and embracing the beauty and power of eros, but knowing that, as rich and rewarding as sexual love is, it's not the final goal of any spiritual quest.

Dante's meeting with Bernard isn't the first time the Song of Songs plays a role in the *Comedy*. Entering Paradise with Beatrice by his side, the dream of *La Vita Nuova* come true at last, he hears chants from the Song of Songs: "Come with me from Lebanon, my bride." At a moment when Dante hasn't fully understood that agape is the wellspring of all love, he hears the Song as a celebration of his personal desires, the deep eros he feels for his beloved. By the time Beatrice returns to her place, he has fully accepted eros's place in the larger harmony. Redirecting Dante's gaze from Beatrice to Mary, "for whom I am all aflame with love," Bernard ushers him into the place for which philia and eros have prepared him: the innermost circles of Paradise, where souls who once shared Dante's struggles live in harmony with the love that guides the universe.

In that place of pure, brilliant clarity, known as the Empyrean, Dante sees the saints gathered in the form of a rose, long a Christian symbol for divine love. Men, women, children are all present in recognizable form, their variety of age and sex not obscured in this realm, but no longer a basis for any kind of hierarchy or oppression. Their unity in the adoration of God is symbolized by Eve, blamed for humanity's downfall, sitting companionably at Mary's feet. Bernard points Dante to the two women, noting, "The wound that Mary closed and anointed," by giving birth to God's Son, "she at her feet who is so fair, it was that opened and pierced it." Eve and Mary aren't opposites, one damned and the other blessed— whore and virgin, sinner and saint, and other misogynist dichotomies. They're jointly mothers of humankind, united in agape for eternity.

It's to Mary, most blessed of all the saints, that St. Bernard prays as he prepares Dante to lay eyes on God, a daunting prospect for any mortal. "From the nethermost pits of the universe to here," Bernard prays, Dante "has seen one by one the lives of the spirits." Now he needs motherly help to "disperse . . . every cloud of his mortality" so that his eyes will be able to see what the re-born saints see: God's own self. That vision will be, as Dante says, "the end of all desires," which will put an end to "the ardor of my craving." The end of all desires: their original purpose and culmination, leading to a state of peaceful joy that echoes the prayer Augustine offers God in the first paragraph of his *Confessions:* "You arouse us so that praising you may bring us joy, because you have made us and drawn us to yourself, and our heart is restless until it rests in you."

That state of rest is shared, bringing philia into harmony with agape. The souls in Paradise are doing what they were born to do: live in the love of God, with each other. They're still who they were when they were alive, still recognizable persons. But they're not conflicted anymore; they're not individualistic, jealous, insecure. They can love fully, because they have arrived at the place where all the loves join and become marvelously indistinguishable from each other. Their desires are extinguished, but that's not because they're not allowed to have desires, or are forced to repress them. It's because their deepest desires, their greatest loves, have been *fulfilled* in a way that honors each person, connects them with every other soul, and grounds them deeply, beyond human imagining, in the source of all life and love.

When Dante the pilgrim arrives in the Empyrean, his poetic craft deserts him. He warns his readers, "From that moment my vision was greater than our speech, which fails at such a sight." As he writes, Dante appeals directly to God, the "Light Supreme," for some measure of skill to return so that he can share the vision he has received. What arrives is a pair of metaphorical images. First, Dante perceives God as an all-encompassing book, containing everything in the universe "bound by love in one volume." That vision is appropriate for a poet, and for a God who communicates with people through sacred texts, but as Dante continues to gaze upon the book, it's displaced by a second image. It's not God who has changed, but Dante whose eyes have gained strength, and who now sees the Divine as three interlocking, harmonious circles:

"the one seemed reflected by the other as rainbow by rainbow, and the third seemed fire breathed forth equally from the one and the other."

Dante's vision is deeply trinitarian, as is appropriate for a Christian poet, but it couldn't be farther from the tired Christian trope of portraying Father, Son, and Holy Spirit as old man, young man, and dove (better known as the "two men and a bird" model). The mystery that lies at the heart of divinity is preserved in Dante's vision, but there's room for humanity too: within the circling light he perceives a reflection "painted with our likeness." How, exactly, humanity can be so intimately cradled within divinity is a mystery, akin to "the squaring of the circle," which "for all the [mathematician's] thinking" can't be solved. That's all right, because solving the mystery of love isn't the point. Rejoicing in it is.

Dante's gift to the world is expressed in his first vision of God: he gave us a book that more beautifully than any other describes the journey from alienation, through awareness, to deep connection. His "desire and will" unified "like a wheel revolving uniformly," his eyes fixed on the "love that moves the sun and the other stars," Dante found the answer to the question of what he truly wanted. It wasn't to sleep with Beatrice, but to write a book that explores the ever-widening circles of interlocking eros, agape and philia.

Others have followed in his footsteps, writing stories that elaborate these truths, pointing us away from Hell, inviting us to walk through Purgatory together, and reveling in the patches of Paradise we encounter along the way. These artists know that the stories we tell matter deeply: we need to imagine them, share them, and live their lessons in our lives. They also know there's always a distance between the best stories we can imagine, and our attempts to live by their wisdom. The promise of the *Divine Comedy* is that the distance isn't impassable, that our desires don't have to destroy us, that we can channel the creative power of all of the loves.

But, as Shakespeare well knew, there are times when it seems we'll never get out of Hell.

Shakespeare

CHAPTER TWO

"Shakespeare's Blues, or, 'How Did I End Up in Hell, and Why Is It So Hard To Get Out?'"

Jealousy, obsession, self-delusion, isolation. Violence, depression, regret. Missed opportunities, wasted lives. There's no aspect of eros gone bad that Shakespeare didn't know. Even as he celebrated the glories of sexual love, he was haunted by the knowledge of how quickly the dream of fulfillment could dissolve amidst demonic laughter. "Th'expense of spirit in a waste of shame is lust in action," he wrote in Sonnet 129. In the cold light of the morning after, the consequences of our sexual obsessions obliterate their imagined pleasures. "Before a joy proposed; behind, a dream," lust is "perjured, murd'rous, bloody, full of blame." As we live out our mundane variations on *Romeo and Juliet* and *Othello*, our reflections gaze out from Shakespeare's mirror: "All this the world well knows, yet none knows well, to shun the heaven that leads men to this hell."

Eros turned to lust can imprison us in the psychic room sketched by the speaker of Sonnet 138. Involved in a compulsive affair with a younger lover, he accepts her protestations of faithfulness with ironic self-contempt: "When my love swears she is made of truth, I do believe her, though I know she lies." He settles for physical gratification, accepting his place in a story built on deceit: "Therefore I lie with her, and she with me, And in our faults by lies we flattered be." The emotional climate is as cold as the deepest circles of Dante's Inferno.

Shakespeare immerses us in a world disquietingly like our own. Like the characters in his plays, we accept stock roles in erotic dramas we don't really want to live. Entranced by a beautiful face, a gesture, or a scent, we forget the ties that bind and let momentary desires lead us to places we never should have gone. Lacerated by jealousy, we strike out in wounded rage, not bothering to cross-check our fears against the facts. We swear eternal loyalty but vanish with the next gust of wind. Cornered, we lie. Sometimes we pause in the middle of an argument, sensing that we're speaking someone else's lines, instead of listening to our own heart and to the person we're talking to—not a cardboard villain, but another human being whom, just yesterday, we loved.

The problem is deeply personal, but it's not just an individual lack of self-awareness or self-control. In our time, as in Shakespeare's, everyone shares the responsibility for eros gone wrong. Lovers who lock themselves away from the world; churches full of sinners who condemn them; friends who turn away from the carnage mouthing incantations to absolve themselves of blame: *"he needs to get his act together," "it's none of my business," "how can she let that go on?"* Too often we avoid difficult conversations, shying away from the hard work of philia. Spectators in an audience that doesn't realize it's part of the play, we reassure ourselves there was nothing we could have done, as tragedies unwind to their foregone bitter ends.

Shakespeare was fully aware that bitterness wasn't the whole story. He felt the pull of eros in the deepest recesses of his soul, and he reveled in its defiance of social convention. He never tired of the titillating possibilities provided by young male actors playing young women who disguise themselves as young men, seducing men and women alike. Antony and Cleopatra exchange clothes and, presumably, sexual roles. Deep in our erotic beings, Shakespeare says with a knowing wink, none of us is quite who we seem.

Literary critic Terry Eagleton has observed that Shakespeare's language is itself a creative, erotic force constantly straining against bourgeois propriety. His vocabulary of 17,000 words dwarfs that of the King James Bible (7000 words) or the average speaker of cultivated English (4000 words); the Oxford English Dictionary credits him with adding 3000 words to the language. That linguistic richness fuels the erotic joy his characters experience. Juliet casts herself into the sea of language and love with equal measures of humor and hormones. "Give me my Romeo," she swoons, "and when I shall die, Take him and cut him out in little stars, And he will make the face of heaven so fine, That all the world will be in love with night." The hard-nosed Roman soldier Enobarbus turns lyric poet when he describes Cleopatra. The wind is lovesick in her presence; lying in her pavilion, surrounded by a "strange invisible perfume," she "o'erpictures" the goddess Venus; her beauty "beggar[s] all description." Enobarbus's reluctant praise rivals Dante's offerings to Beatrice as the most lavish compliment any woman has ever received: "Age cannot wither her, nor custom stale her infinite variety."

But even in his sunniest moments, Shakespeare knew the sky could darken in a heartbeat. Seen from a slightly different angle, the comic disguises that make room for erotic play morph into the sinister masks of a world where no one can be trusted and nothing is as it seems. Case in point: *Romeo and Juliet*. If you suppress your knowledge of how things turn out, the first two acts play like a variation on *As You Like It* or *Twelfth Night*. Exuberant young men wander in the moonlight, sharing their dreams. Enchanted and enchanting teenagers improvise a perfect sonnet on first meeting. The heroine guides her lust-blinded suitor gently towards an understanding that love is more than fantasy and flowery speeches. In the hands of a good cast, the sweet, sexy balcony scene isn't a cliché. But then Mercutio and Tybalt are killed and the fulcrum shifts. The destructive face of eros emerges from behind the comic mask.

In this chapter, we use the vocabulary of the three loves to explain how and why that happens. Looking at Shakespeare's world through our lens brings the picture into sharp focus: divorced from philia and agape, eros can't resist the social and psychological forces that twist it to their own ends. In the tragedies—but also, as we'll show, in comedies like *A Midsummer Night's Dream*—the three loves are warped almost beyond recognition. Eros is a commodity, something to be controlled and exploited. Philia and agape are little more than rhetorical gestures. Lovers fail to talk; friends withdraw; religion is a pawn in a political game. Shakespeare fully comprehended the creative power of eros, but he understood equally well that, when the harmony among the three loves breaks down, it can become a destructive force that won't take us anywhere but Hell.

Shakespeare and/in Love

In Shakespeare's England, that breakdown was a central fact of life. At the turn of the seventeenth century, when his career was nearing its peak, London was a center of both the global capitalism that was just swinging into full gear and the newly profitable commercial theater. In that physically, emotionally, and financially risky environment, philia was under severe pressure. Communities came together quickly, and just as rapidly dissolved. Friendships were subject to strict social regulation, largely but not exclusively based on class. Shakespeare's relationship with Henry Wriothesley, the third Earl of Southampton, is a prime example. There's a consensus among Shakespeareans that Southampton is the "Fair Youth" celebrated in the poet's first 17 sonnets. Many believe him to be the "master-mistress of my passion" of Sonnet 20, an erotically charged celebration of androgynous beauty. Without question, strong bonds of affection connected the poet and the young aristocrat to whom he dedicated two long poems, including the erotic tour-de-force *Venus and Adonis*. But, however intense their connection, Shakespeare remained Southampton's social inferior, a fact clearly evident in the dedication to *The Rape of Lucrece*. "The love I dedicate to your lordship is without end," he begins. "What I have done is yours, what I have to do is yours, being part in all I have, devoted yours. Were my worth greater, my duty would show greater." The subordination of love to duty would emerge as a central theme in many of Shakespeare's greatest plays. However powerful love's pull might be, it was always conditioned by issues of power and rank.

Nor could the possibilities for philia be separated from the challenges facing agape. In this period, self-sacrificial, compassionate love seemed divorced from the church, and no institution of any significant social presence offered an alternative vision. Elizabeth I had ushered in a period of relative religious calm with her church "settlement" one year after Shakespeare's birth, striking a middle ground between Catholicism and Protestantism while reinforcing her authority as head of the Church of England. Despite the superficial calm, contentious debates over theology and worship, as well as the secret practice of Catholicism, continued through Shakespeare's lifetime. The possibility of religious wars at home and abroad wasn't abstract, as evidenced by Elizabeth's execution of Mary, the Catholic Queen of Scotland, when Shakespeare was a young man. The issue came into sharp focus for Shakespeare when Southampton, who belonged to a prominent Catholic family, narrowly escaped execution for his part in the abortive revolt against Elizabeth led by the Earl of Essex.

In that environment, love in all its forms was under siege. The theater was a battleground and Shakespeare was one of the conflict's chief, and most wily, warriors. Like any astute person of his time, he knew that even seemingly innocuous gestures—love stories that could be seen as political allegories, or seemingly trivial slights against a patron, the crown, or the church—could send one hurtling back down the social ladder or worse, into prison. That political danger may be one reason why we know so little about Shakespeare's experience or personal opinions. Even when he wrote plays on controversial subjects such as the deposition of a monarch (*Richard II*), Shakespeare was careful to distance them from contemporary events. His religious affiliation remains a source of controversy; his family had Catholic roots, but adhered at least outwardly to the Church of England. Well-known examples reminded Shakespeare of the consequences for those who failed to walk the tightrope: the murder of his rival playwright and friend Christopher Marlowe, which may or may not have been the result of his involvement in political intrigues; and the imprisonment of poet John Donne for marrying his patron's young ward without her father's consent.

While Shakespeare's language overflowed with eros, his life appears to have been a model of caution and restraint, lived largely in accord with the bourgeois conventions he lampooned in his plays. The son of a glove-maker who became mayor of Stratford-upon-Avon but whose financial fortunes rose and fell, Shakespeare received a good grammar school education, and had many chances to see visiting theater troupes. He married young and established his wife and children at the family residence in Stratford before moving to London to launch what would be, in both financial and artistic terms, an extremely successful career. Investing wisely in himself, his theater company, and London real estate, Shakespeare accumulated sufficient wealth to retire at age 46.

Unaware of, or uninterested in this evidence, battalions of bardolators, including platoons of otherwise sober academics, have decided that Shakespeare's portraits of human passion *must* be drawn from life. His plays are so vivid, and communicate so much about eros, that the temptation to hallucinate his life into a love story has proven irresistible. The most extreme, influential, and entertaining expression of that desire is the 1998 film *Shakespeare in Love*, a take-off on *Romeo and Juliet* that sets the playwright himself, imagined as a cross between Clark Gable and Woody Allen, at the center of the original star-crossed love affair. The film won seven Academy Awards including Best Picture, beating out Steven Spielberg's famously bloody drama *Saving Private Ryan* in a contest of love vs. war. The appeal of *Shakespeare in Love* goes beyond the radiant good looks and magnetism of Gwyneth Paltrow and Joseph Fiennes in the lead roles, or Judi Dench's portrayal of a majestic yet crotchety Queen Elizabeth. The film allows viewers with a high-school familiarity with Shakespeare the fun of imagining they have inside knowledge of his genius. Who knows?—*Shakespeare in Love* suggests—maybe pillow debates with a girlfriend about whether the night owl or the morning rooster was vocalizing outside the window were the real inspiration for Romeo and Juliet's lyrical flights with the nightingale and the lark.

On a slightly more scholarly level, an ever-expanding shelf of speculative biographies indulges readers with the juicier, and entirely hypothetical, details of Shakespeare's erotic life. Starved for evidence, critics and readers transform the sonnets into confessional poetry, creating narratives that can be neither proved nor disproved. According to various sources, Shakespeare had affairs with an impressive number of women and men, beginning in his teens with Anne Hathaway, usually cast as an older woman who seduced the bard-to-be into marriage six months before the birth of a daughter. At one time or another, Shakespeare has been sexually or romantically linked with Christopher Marlowe, the Earls of Southampton and Pembroke, the boy actor William Hughes, the wives and mistresses of most of his friends and colleagues, every prostitute mentioned in the historical record, and a dizzying array of "Dark Ladies," including the courtier Mary Fitton, the Countess of Southampton Elizabeth Wriothesley, and the "black Jewess" Emilia Lanier (*née* Bassano), whom a few have credited with actually writing his works.

Barring the invention of time travel, the speculation about Shakespeare's biography is going to remain just that. Ultimately, the details of his personal life don't matter; his plays endure, testifying to his genius as a student of human behavior. They're the reason that, the same year *Shakespeare in Love* cleaned up at the Oscars, listeners of BBC Radio voted Shakespeare the "British Person of the Millennium." For a change, a survey got it right. It would take a committee of scientists like Isaac Newton and Stephen Hawking, philosophers like John Locke and Mary Wollstonecraft, and politicians like Queen Victoria and Winston Churchill, to match Shakespeare's ability to touch ordinary lives with his emotional and intellectual wisdom. That wisdom shone most brightly when he turned to the challenges, joys, and—above all—dangers of love.

Labyrinth of Lies: *Othello*

Nowhere is the destructive power of eros more obvious than in *Othello*. Warped from the beginning in a toxic brew of misogyny and racism laced with jealousy, the erotic love between Othello and Desdemona never has a chance to flower into a life-giving force. Destructive scripts play out to their foreseeable ends as Iago and Roderigo manipulate philia, and Othello loses faith in everything and everyone: his wife, his friends, himself. Desdemona alone holds to a shred of agape, but, reduced to an object in the minds of the men around her, she lacks the power to change the tragic scenario. Her maid, Iago's wife Emilia, sounds a note of practical realism, but in this Hell ruled by rumor and slander there's no room for anything resembling reason. Both women die at their husbands' hands while speaking truths about love the men can't bear to hear.

It's all too easy to translate *Othello* to modern settings. The film *All Night Long* makes Othello the leader of a jazz band in 1960s London; *Catch My Soul*, starring singers Richie Havens and Tony Joe White, relocates the action to the New Mexico desert. One of most successful adaptations, *O* updates the play as the story of a black high school basketball star's relationship with the daughter of the white dean. No big-city newspaper goes a week without reporting the grisly details of a love triangle, real or imagined, ending in bloodshed.

Contemplating these examples and the original play itself, one question persists: *why* does eros draw Othello and everyone around him so quickly into Hell? Many explanations focus on the villain Iago, whose stated goal is to destroy Othello. But not even he seems to believe his declared motives: anger at having been passed over for a promotion, and an almost certainly baseless suspicion that Othello has committed adultery with Emilia. Others explain the tragedy as the result of racism, or some ultimately unfathomable principle of malice. Neither approach is wrong, but both miss the deeper insights into eros that emerge when we consider the characters' interlocking, but mutually unintelligible, actions in relation to the three loves. The men's self-images depend on the commodification of women, still a familiar phenomenon in our day, from locker room to board room. Philia and eros are warped into tools that render honesty, loving connections, and faith nearly impossible; the characters accept their place in scenarios based on stereotypes, competition, and fear.

Lust—the warped form of eros—motivates almost everyone: Iago; Othello; Desdemona's possessive father Brabantio; the inept chump Roderigo, who wants Desdemona for himself; Othello's lieutenant Cassio, whom Iago casts in the role of Desdemona's illicit lover; and Bianca, Cassio's mistress. From the opening scene, jealousy and objectification rule the characters and their actions: almost all of them want control over someone—something—they can't have. In the opening scene, Roderigo and Iago rouse Brabantio out of bed with cries of "Thieves, thieves!" They proceed to stir him into a frenzy with the image of "an old black ram" mating with "your white ewe." Iago's strategy is based on the erotic fantasies and jealous projections he knows Othello, Brabantio, and Cassio have in their heads. He plays the other men against each other in a high-stakes game, cynically guessing how they will respond to his cues. They don't disappoint him.

Othello's concept of philia is limited by his simplistic notions of male bonding and his inability to imagine women as anything other than erotic objects. Placing uncritical trust in his men's loyalty, he fails to realize Iago is manipulating them all. Because he places philia and eros in separate spheres, Othello never considers talking with Desdemona about Iago's accusations; she's his lover, not his friend. Caught up in an erotic nightmare, with nowhere to turn for help, he drags everyone into Hell as Iago lures him on.

The play's action revolves around a mundane object: Desdemona's handkerchief, an heirloom that once belonged to Othello's mother and was his first gift to his wife. When Desdemona drops the handkerchief without noticing, Iago picks it up and makes it the centerpiece of his plot. At first Othello refuses to believe Iago's insinuations that Desdemona has been unfaithful with Cassio, demanding "ocular proof" that "my love [is] a whore." Using one of the now-common phrases that Shakespeare coined, Iago cynically warns Othello, "O, beware, my lord, of jealousy! It is the green-eyed monster which doth mock the meat it feeds on." He provides "evidence," claiming to have seen Cassio wipe his beard with the missing handkerchief. Othello demands that Desdemona produce it, and when she can't, he confronts her with his mother's warning that the handkerchief was charmed, and that "if she lost it, or made a gift of it, my father's eye should hold her loathed." Desdemona's desperate denial that she has lost the handkerchief feeds Iago's scheme.

For the men in the play, Desdemona might as well be the missing handkerchief: an object for her husband to value and display as long as he believes she belongs to him alone, a thing for the men around him to manipulate for their own ends. Among the characters, only Desdemona resists the destructive script Iago is exploiting, but she's powerless to escape its outcome. She invokes agape sincerely, but receives no support from anyone around her, not even her maid Emilia, who shares the cynicism about love that permeates their world. Protesting her innocence and the fidelity of women in general, Desdemona asks Emilia, "Dost thou in conscience think... that there be women do abuse their husbands in such gross kind?" Emilia offers a brief, clear reality check: "There be some such, no question." When Desdemona protests "by this heavenly light" that she wouldn't betray Othello, Emilia answers in a tone of gently comic realism, "Nor I neither, by this heavenly light. I might do't as well i' th'dark." When an incredulous Desdemona asks, "Wouldst thou do such a thing for all the world?" Emilia provides an honest, world-weary answer. The world, she says, "is a great price for a small vice." "Who would not make her husband a cuckold to make him a monarch?" she asks, even though she knows Desdemona counts herself among those women.

Even as she denies Desdemona's romanticized vision of female fidelity, Emilia makes an implicitly feminist case for women's equality and men's culpability. Women are justified in taking offense, and revenge, when their husbands abuse them or are unfaithful themselves. In fidelity and infidelity, women are no more or less human than their men: "have not we affections, desires for sport, and frailty, as men have?" For Emilia, the human potential for rising above appetites, for sex or revenge, is limited or nonexistent. Despite the fact that she's a more sympathetic character than her conniving husband, Emilia stands on a slippery ethical slope, where only a short step separates her utilitarian vision from his amoral view of the world. Desdemona alone continues to hope for redemption, praying God will show her how, "Not to pick bad from bad"—not to emulate men's bad behavior—but "by bad mend." That is, to let the transgressors in her circles spur her to set a better example.

In this deepest circle of Shakespeare's Hell, the view of agape that wins out is Iago's: there simply is no such thing. He dismisses any moral authority beyond the individual himself (and for Iago, the individual who gets to construct his own moral universe *is* a "him"). When Roderigo confesses that he dotes on Desdemona too much, "but it is not in my virtue" to change, Iago responds contemptuously: "Virtue? A fig!" The master schemer could be speaking from the bowels of Dante's Inferno when he asserts the individual's right to follow his will wherever it leads. "Our bodies are our gardens," he declares, "to the which our wills are gardeners. So that if we will plant nettles or sow lettuce, set up hyssop and weed up thyme . . . why the power and corrigible authority of this lies in our wills." Neither human friendship nor divine guidance checks that will. Unlike Virgil, who counseled a confused Dante that "love must be the seed in you of every virtue and of every action deserving punishment," Iago invokes a warped form of "reason" as the tamer of the will, while simultaneously manipulating his victims' half-conscious erotic desires. "We have reason to cool our raging motions, our carnal stings, our unbitted lusts"—his dismissive description of the feelings Roderigo calls love. Love has no place in Iago's map of the psyche, either as the source of human actions or their goal.

For Iago, Desdemona's virtue and her faith in agape amount to little more than easily vanquished pawns in a contest of wills—a contest only Iago knows is happening, and one he's determined to win. In that battle, he can't see Othello's love for Desdemona as anything other than a weapon at her disposal: "His soul is so enfettered to her love that she may make, unmake, do what she list." Distorting agape beyond recognition, he observes that her erotic power allows her to "play the god" over her husband. Even as Iago justifies his manipulation of the men around him, he knows his arguments reflect a Satanic logic. Muttering "Divinity of hell!" he plots to make Desdemona's compassion her downfall by turning it to his own advantage. As she pleads to Othello for Cassio's reinstatement as his lieutenant, Iago vows to "pour this pestilence into his ear," telling him that Desdemona intercedes for Cassio not out of friendship, but to keep her illicit lover nearby to appease "her body's lust."

In the absence of philia, agape, and a rich, full eros, that motivation seems all too plausible to her husband. Desdemona only realizes what's happened when Othello is about to murder her, citing "honest Iago's" guidance in what he still can't see is a labyrinth of lies. When Desdemona cries, "Alas, [Cassio] is betrayed, and I undone," Othello takes her tears of grief as a personal insult. He won't even allow her a final prayer of preparation for death before smothering her with her own pillow. As Desdemona lingers between life and death, she refuses to accuse her husband of her murder, saying that she herself is responsible, but that "A guiltless death I die." Even then, Othello can't accept her offering of agape, exclaiming to a stunned Emilia, "She's like a liar gone to burning hell! 'Twas I that killed her."

In that godforsaken mess—or to state it more accurately, the mess created when people act solely on their immediate desires—no forgiveness or redemption is possible. Emilia, the first person to deduce the whole truth about what has transpired, is murdered by her husband for speaking it. Even at the end of the play, when a stunned Othello has learned the depths of Iago's treachery and his own blindness, and has decided to kill himself, he defends his actions by claiming, "naught I did in hate, but all in honour." Love, with its honest but difficult demands, and wonderful if hard-won rewards, ultimately has no place in this Hell. The play's action is driven by concerns over reputation, social place; the characters are unable to escape the roles society has assigned. Without love, the supposed prizes are empty shells, and worse: as the play ends, the stage is littered with dead bodies and Iago is led away to be executed. The absence of love is not only "chaos," as Othello cries out when he first starts to doubt Desdemona. It's death.

Fallen Angels: *Measure for Measure*

Othello presents an extreme, if familiar, vision of the deadly mixture of libido, jealousy, and the desire to control a lover. In *Measure for Measure*, Shakespeare gives us a subtler version of the ways lust insinuates itself into the fabric of everyday life. As in most erotic debacles, no one dies, but that doesn't mean the damage done is any less real. Set in a city where Emilia's cynicism provides the rulebook for a game no one acknowledges but everyone plays, *Measure* poses a question that resonates in the twenty-first century. In a world where eros is imagined either as a commodity to be exploited, or a force to be repressed, what happens to the few people who seek a better way, and refuse to utter their lines as scripted? Shakespeare's response isn't encouraging. In this circle of the moral Inferno, the only person who attempts to keep the loves in balance finds herself trapped between competing and irreconcilable notions of philia and agape, unable to find a path out.

The plot of *Measure for Measure* reads like a "family values" nightmare. It's familiar from our own time, when each successive revelation that a fundamentalist preacher or moralizing politician has been consorting with prostitutes barely qualifies as news. The curtain rises on the Duke of Vienna in despair over the moral laxity in his domain, the sexual license and commercialization symbolized by the brothels on every street corner. Aware that his own leniency has contributed to the problem, the duke rationalizes that he can't suddenly change course: "'twas my fault to give the people scope, 'twould be my tyranny to strike and gall them" now. He announces that he's going on a long journey, empowering his regent Angelo, a man with a reputation for moral rectitude, "to enforce or qualify the laws as to your soul seems good." Disguising himself as a friar in order to stay close by and observe his people's behavior, the duke puts on the garb of agape, but evades the hard work and honesty that philia requires.

Angelo embodies the contradictions of the repressive attitude toward eros, turning a blind eye to its goodness, and to the ways his own actions warp it into a destructive force. Self-righteously reducing agape to a list of "thou shall nots" with correspondingly harsh punishments, he resolves to enforce Vienna's law against fornication. The rigidity of his attitude is underlined by his choice of a test case: Claudio, a young man who has gotten his fiancée Julietta pregnant. Claudio and Julietta consider themselves married, and are only waiting for her dowry to increase before formalizing their vows. In other words, as couples through the ages have done, they're delaying marriage until they can afford it. They're nowhere close to the worst offenders in a town where the streets are jammed with men eager to have sex and move on, among them Claudio's friend Lucio, who has fathered a child with a prostitute, Kate Keepdown, then lied about it so he wouldn't have to marry her. Under arrest, Claudio defends himself to Lucio: "Upon a true contract I got possession of Julietta's bed. You know the lady. She is fast my wife, Save that we do the denunciation [i.e., proclamation] lack of outward order." Normally, with Julietta due to give birth soon, the couple should be able to remedy their situation by marrying legally—gaining the "outward order" they lacked. But the inflexible Angelo adheres to the letter of the law and orders Claudio executed the next day. For Shakespeare, whose wife gave birth six months after their wedding, the situation struck close to home.

Claudio's prospects are bleak. Only two people can free or condemn him: the duke, whose disguise keeps him from exercising power on Claudio's behalf; and Angelo, whose actions are grounded in a religious judgment that's unalloyed by mercy. To plead for Claudio in the voice of agape, Shakespeare introduces his sister Isabella, a complex character who has been interpreted as everything from Shakespeare's emblem of purity to a monster who demands that her brother die for her convictions. Viewing Isabella in relation to the three loves provides a way of understanding her as a voice of agape speaking a language no one around her understands. Repelled by the moral cesspool she has grown up observing, she has become a novice in a convent of St. Clare. Unquestionably sincere in her vocation, she wants to live a life that embodies love for God, and the Sisters of St. Clare seem to offer it. When we first meet her, she tells a senior nun that she desires, not greater freedom, but "a more strict restraint Upon the sisterhood." Isabella hasn't yet realized that the convent remains a part of the messy world she's trying to escape, in which there are few black-and-white solutions to love's infinite dilemmas. As the play progresses and she's put in a position to choose between her brother and God, Isabella's impulse is to treat the choice as clear-cut, but Shakespeare shows it to be extremely—maybe irresolvably—complex.

When Lucio visits the convent to inform Isabella of her brother and Julietta's predicament, she has a ready solution: "O, let him marry her!" Granted an audience with Angelo, she asks him to free Claudio, and finds that he doesn't share her assumptions about the appropriate response to sin. For Angelo, the divine power that legitimizes his secular office is expressed through clear-cut judgment, not mercy. In his hands, agape has been warped into a tool for the exercise of power over others. Isabella, whose relationship to God isn't based on personal advantage, is stunned by the regent's implacability and challenges him as a fellow sinner: "How would you be if He which is the top of judgment should but judge you as you are?" Angelo doesn't engage with her argument; rather, he absolves himself of any responsibility: "It is the law, not I, condemn your brother." Angelo's judgmentalism turns a deaf ear to true agape's plea for forgiveness and a fresh start.

Shakespeare underscores the bankruptcy of Angelo's position when the regent removes the mask of impartial interpreter of the law and offers Isabella Claudio's life in exchange for sex. He has already wondered to himself why he finds Isabella's virtue so enticing, asking, "Dost thou desire her foully for those things that make her good?" It's a mindset familiar to the twentieth- and twenty-first-century pornographers for whom images of despoiled purity are a stock-in-trade. To Isabella, however, Angelo presents the matter as a simple transaction. Reminding her that he holds the key to her brother's freedom, he asks if "there were no earthly mean to save him but that either you must lay down the treasures of your body . . . or else to let him suffer. What would you do?" Isabella answers in an instant, keeping eternity in mind: her brother's death would be "the cheaper way. Better it were a brother died at once than that a sister, by redeeming him, should die forever." When she threatens to "tell the world aloud what man thou art," Angelo replies, "Who will believe thee, Isabel?" It will be her word against his: one of power's oldest, most destructive ploys.

Shakespeare presents Isabella's choice as less clear-cut than it seems to her. Holding fast to her moral code even when she sees Claudio in prison, Isabella tells her brother to prepare for death. Desperate, he pleads with her in the name of philia: "Sweet sister, let me live. What sin you do to save a brother's life, nature dispenses with the deed so far that it becomes a virtue." Prostitution in the defense of her brother's liberty, he implies, would be no vice. If Claudio refuses to see the impossibility of his sister's position, Isabella, for her part, has no way to respond that would honor both philia and agape. Her outraged response shows no sympathy: "Is't not a kind of incest to take life from thine own sister's shame?" Her use of the term "shame" raises the question: is she more concerned with preserving her honor—appearances and social standing—than with truly virtuous conduct? If the latter, is she overstating the risk to her soul if she gave in to Angelo's demand; would God or the church really hold her morally responsible when her brother's life hung in the balance? No simple formula—no law—can resolve the siblings' dilemma. Isabella wants to affirm the erotic bond between her brother and Julietta, but the law—as written and as interpreted by Angelo—makes that impossible.

The libidinous dodge Angelo proposes would reduce her to her body and it to a commodity. When Isabella tells Claudio of the proposal, his first response is to recoil. "O heavens, it cannot be!" he cries out. "Thou shalt not do't." Unlike Isabella, however, Claudio has no trust in the next life. Speaking a vivid, dramatically powerful language that has the potential to dominate the stage and overshadow the complications at hand, he paints a picture of death that rivals Dante's in its intensity, but in which Heaven has no place. "Ay, but to die and go we know not where, To lie in cold obstruction and to rot, This sensible warm motion to become A kneaded clod; and the delighted spirit To breathe in fiery flood, or to reside In thrilling region of thick-ribbed ice." Caught up in existential panic, he urges her to make the trade. By herself, Isabella can't find a third way out of this death trap that would honor all the loves.

Shakespeare never resolves this tension. Instead, he provides a comic solution by pulling a rabbit—the disguised duke—out of his playwright's hat. Paying Isabella a chaste compliment, "The hand that hath made you fair hath made you good," the duke-friar offers her a damning story from Angelo's past. Some time earlier, the regent had broken his engagement to a local woman, Mariana, on the pretext that she had been unfaithful. But the duke reveals the real reason: Mariana's dowry had been lost at sea when her brother's ship wrecked. Angelo had "Left her in her tears and dried not one of them with his comfort, swallowed his vows whole." In a variation on the "bed trick," a familiar literary device from the biblical story of Leah and Rachel to numerous Renaissance comedies, he proposes that Isabella agree to meet the regent but that Mariana take her place in the dark. After Isabella agrees to the plan and leaves, the duke-friar offers the audience a justification for his plot: "He who the sword of heaven will bear, should be as holy as severe . . . More nor less to others paying than by self-offenses weighing." Those who judge will be judged, measure for measure.

The trap works as planned. Isabella tells Mariana the story, and Mariana has sex with Angelo while pretending to be a veiled Isabella. The duke-friar fakes Claudio's death, leaving Angelo to believe that not only has he raped Isabella, but now he can't keep his end of their bargain. He can only regret his actions, believing it's too late to remedy them, and bemoaning how far he has fallen: "Alack, when once our grace we have forgot, Nothing goes right." Today, his next step would be the televised press conference, complete with tears, contorted rationalizations, and unconvincing remorse.

The play's ending unfolds quickly. Isabella accuses Angelo and is arrested for slander; Mariana testifies that Angelo is her husband in the carnal sense; and the duke exposes Angelo's lies with the knowledge he gained while disguised as the friar. The duke orders Angelo and Mariana married. When the duke immediately sentences Angelo to death, in accord with the law the regent has so strictly enforced, Isabella joins Mariana in pleading for his life, arguing that his "bad intent" "must be buried but as an intent that perished by the way." Angelo would have dismissed that argument out of hand, but the duke yields, pardoning Angelo along with Claudio, who's brought out of hiding.

The play's dénouement has left generations of spectators to wonder whether it's a tragedy or a comedy. Critics often duck the issue by declaring it one of Shakespeare's "problem plays." The core of the problem, which the lens of the three loves brings into focus, is that *Measure for Measure* leaves in place all the tensions that generated Isabella's dilemma. Angelo has been revealed as a hypocrite, but there's no sense that Vienna's future will be any different from its past. The brothels have moved underground, but their headquarters will be reopening as soon as the political winds shift back. At the duke's order, Lucio marries Kate Keepdown; the fact that he neither loves nor respects his bride, the mother of his child, is irrelevant. Although Mariana gets her wish to marry Angelo, she has to live with the knowledge that her husband broke his vow to her when it no longer served his economic interest, and then tried to use political power to buy another woman's body. Not exactly a fairy-tale ending.

The duke gives no sign that he's capable of leading his people to a deeper understanding of agape or philia, or that, rhetoric aside, he sees eros as anything more than an item for sale at the best possible price. Although he claims the moral high ground in lifting the two men's death sentences, he echoes Angelo's offer to Isabella in only slightly loftier terms: "for your sake is he pardoned; and for your lovely sake, give me your hand, and say you will be mine . . ." Like Angelo, the duke assumes Isabella can be bought. The only difference between the two men is that the duke asks for more of her time—their whole lives instead of one night—and offers a different form of payment—his wealth instead of her brother's life.

The text of *Measure for Measure* provides no clue about Isabella's response. Most productions treat the ending as a comedy, bringing Isabella and the duke together in a romantic embrace. Others maintain the uncertainty, bringing down the curtain on the motionless pair. A few actresses turn away in disgust, leaving us with an Isabella whose sole desire is to return to the convent. Even that interpretation leaves questions unanswered: is she embracing agape or fleeing eros? In a world where the duke holds ultimate power, does she really have a choice?

The play's title doesn't answer these questions, but it does point to a moral center amidst the murkiness. Both caution and promise, "measure for measure" may be drawn from Jesus' warning in Matthew's Gospel, "Judge not, that ye be not judged. For with what judgment ye judge, ye shall be judged: and with what measure ye mete, it shall be measured to you again." The image recurs in Jesus' invitation in Luke, "Give, and it shall be given unto you; good measure, pressed down, shaken together and running over shall men give into your bosom; for with what measure ye mete, with the same shall men mete to you again." Those sayings would have been deeply familiar to Shakespeare's first audiences, and would have alerted them to the themes of judgment and mercy in the action they were about to watch. Some of the people watching from the ground or cheap seats no doubt hoped that the play would end with a powerful judge being himself judged. The more reflective among the nobility might have heard it as a call to reconsider harsh application of the law to protect their personal interests. Later generations of viewers, conditioned by personal beliefs and the intellectual currents of their times, have located the thematic center variously in Isabella's devotion to God or Claudio's existential angst. What's certain is that the lack of a clear resolution still challenges us to ponder fundamental questions of love and justice. Are we willing to be honest about our desires and our mistakes? Do we hold others to higher standards than we hold ourselves? Are we willing to take the risk of finding ways to connect eros with agape and philia in a world that auctions them off separately? Or do we, like the duke, keep an aloof distance, pretending that we're spectators, not participants? While distance may feel like the safer choice, Shakespeare shows us it's the shorter road to Hell.

Shadows in Fairyland: *A Midsummer Nights' Dream*

Even the sunniest of Shakespeare's comedies are shadowed by the dark side of eros. *A Midsummer Night's Dream* is no exception, despite the fact that almost every production of the play takes its benevolence as a given. The mischievous imp Puck's oft-quoted line, "Lord what fools these mortals be," usually delivered in a tone of amused tolerance, is taken as evidence of a world in which the complications of eros resolve harmoniously. While the celebratory elements are real, they're only part of the story. Shakespeare weaves an *Othello*-like awareness of erotic violence into *Midsummer*'s comic fabric, suggesting that a fully lived and embodied eros is the stuff of dreams, a vision we can only long for and touch momentarily, before waking to our day-to-day lives.

Without question, eros is the play's ruling spirit. *Midsummer* sparkles with vibrant language and rollicking humor, and by its end the lovers have paired off with more or less appropriate partners amidst vows of eternal devotion. The unintentional slapstick of the tradesmen's rehearsals and performance of *Pyramus and Thisbe* matches the most uproarious moments of Charlie Chaplin or Woody Allen, and the Whitmanesque Nick Bottom rivals Falstaff among Shakespeare's lovers of life. Each of the play's four plot strands revolves around eros: the marital squabble between the fairy king and queen Oberon and

Titania; the approaching nuptials of Theseus, the Duke of Athens, and Hippolyta; the confusion of the four young lovers; the "very tragical mirth" of the tradesmen's play-within-a-play. Overlapping, colliding and ricocheting off one another, the four plots create a glorious erotic confusion. Following which young lover is infatuated with whom at any given moment can be a daunting challenge. It's less a romantic triangle than a romantic dodecahedron.

For those without a scorecard, at the start of the play Hermia and Lysander are in love with each other; Helena's smitten with Demetrius, who's obsessed with Hermia. When Puck accidentally sprinkles the love pollen on Lysander and Oberon charms Demetrius, both men redirect their ardor toward Helena, who professes utter and understandable distrust of the suddenly attentive males. Restored to his "real" self at the end of the play, Lysander returns his affections to Hermia, leaving Hermia with the original object of her desire. It's easy to forget that the resolution works only because no one bothers to disenchant Demetrius.

The least conflicted celebrant of eros in *A Midsummer Night's Dream* is the weaver Nick Bottom. When one of his compatriots recoils in horror at the thought of playing the woman's role in the love story the tradesmen hope to stage before the Duke, Bottom volunteers to play both lovers. He is large, he contains multitudes, and he's not in the least disturbed when an ass's head appears on his shoulders. Under the influence of yet another love potion, which makes her fall in love with the first being she sees, Titania is smitten with Bottom, who accepts her adulation as if it's the most natural thing in the world. People's tastes differ and *vive la différence*. Offered the airy music of the fairy's love songs, he states his preference for "a peck of provender," telling Titania, "I could munch your good dry oats." As euphemisms go, not bad.

From the beginning, however, the erotic celebrations take place beneath the shadow of erotic violence. As the play opens, Hermia's father Egeus is appealing to Theseus to help him force his daughter to marry Demetrius despite her openly expressed romantic preference for Lysander. Blatantly asserting his property rights, he tells the duke,

"As she is mine, I may dispose of her. Which shall be either to this gentleman or to her death." Theseus backs him up, advising Hermia that "To you, your father should be as a god . . . To whom you are as but a form in wax, By him imprinted, and within his power To leave the figure or disfigure it." Hermia flees alone to the forest, and when she meets Demetrius there, she confronts him directly with the violence of his desire: "If thou hast slain Lysander in his sleep, Being o'er shoes in blood, plunge in the deep and kill me too."

Erotic violence plays a role in each of the plots. Theseus has literally conquered his bride, the Amazon Queen Hippolyta: "I wooed thee with my sword, And won thy love doing thee injuries." Most productions present the forest as a "green world" in contrast to Theseus's cynical, world-weary court, but it's also filled with erotic conflict. The rift between Oberon and Titania stems from the king's wish to possess the "lovely boy" his queen has "stolen from an Indian king." Unimpressed with her husband's assertion of his rights, Titania employs her sexuality as a weapon: "What, jealous Oberon? Fairies, skip hence. I have forsworn his bed and company." Echoing Hermia's father's claim of patriarchal control—"Tarry, rash wanton. Am I not thy lord?"—Oberon promises revenge: "Thou shalt not from this grove, Till I torment thee for this injury." Even the tradesmen's play hinges on the deaths of Pyramus and Thisbe.

Shakespeare fills the margins of *A Midsummer Night's Dream* with threatening spirits, tormented souls who "willfully themselves exile from light, And must for aye consort with black-browed night." His London audiences would have known that thousands of those souls walked the streets of their city, as they do in our own time. Puck hastens to carry out Oberon's comic plot because he wants to avoid the demonic forces "At whose approach, ghosts wand'ring here and there troop home to churchyards." Backing away from Puck's realism, Oberon responds: "But we are spirits of another sort."

This isn't to transform *A Midsummer Night's Dream* into *Hamlet* or *Macbeth*. Among the shadows that are never fully dispelled, it offers a glimpse of a world where a freer, healing spirit can rule, where love can reach out to seemingly lost souls. The key is to use creative imagination to construct a shared vision of eros and philia in harmony, and persevere in living it out together. Resisting her betrothed's cynicism concerning the "airy nothing" of happy endings, Hippolyta puts great store in the fact that the four young lovers bear witness to one another's dreams: "All their minds transfigured so together, More witnesseth than fancy's images." In isolation, the belief that eros can change the world may be a mark of insanity. Placed at the center of a network of friends, it "grows to something of great constancy," something "strange and admirable."

Eros *is* strange; it *is* admirable. But, Shakespeare warns, by itself it can't banish the shadows. Oberon releases Titania from the spell only after she hands over the changeling boy; Egeus rants on endlessly in his patriarchal rage. Even as the betrothed couples prepare to pass the fortnight until their marriages "in nightly revels and new jollity," Puck reminds us that everything takes place in a world where the graves are "gaping wide" and "fairies run from the presence of the sun, Following darkness like a dream."

As so often, Shakespeare's language is ambiguous: is the dream of darkness reality, or is darkness itself the dream? For that matter, does debating the phrasings, playing jazz riffs on the melodies of comedy and tragedy, even make a difference? Do our imaginings, the dreams of lunatics, lovers and poets, really matter?

Only for Nick Bottom is the answer a resounding "Yes." Awakening after Titania's disenchantment he is, for once in his life, at a loss for words as he tries to tell his friends what has transpired. "I have had a most rare vision. I have had a dream past the wit of man to say what dream it was," he begins. "The eye of man hath not heard, the ear of man hath not seen, man's hand is not able to taste, his tongue to conceive, nor his heart to report what my dream was. I will get Peter Quince to write a ballad of this dream. It shall be called 'Bottom's Dream' because it hath no bottom." When eros touches us, he seems to say, all we can do is wonder at what we have lived, accept it, and return to share our vision with a resisting world.

Romeo and Juliet: Paradise Lost

Like Shakespeare's romantic comedies, the first half of *Romeo and Juliet* treats the foibles of infatuation with tender understanding. The play *feels* light-hearted. Eros permeates the atmosphere; the word play dazzles; the moonlight gleams; young lovers kiss and whisper their dreams; even the swordfights feel more like scuffles between high school rivals than battles capable of drawing real blood. After-prom with a hint of carnival. And then, as so often happens in carnivals, the skull appears from behind the laughing mask. The camera pulls back from the lovers' embrace to reveal the grimy streets of a city in which philia serves power, and agape is little more than a rhetorical game.

Romeo and Juliet adapts effortlessly to different times and places. Anywhere family, racial, national, or any other sort of loyalties draw lines between would-be lovers, the play takes root. Which is to say, everywhere. Magical, heartbreaking and as contemporary as it was when it debuted in 1957, *West Side Story* relocates the Montagues and Capulets—transformed into the Puerto Rican Sharks and the "American" Jets—to mid-twentieth-century Manhattan. A 2009 Spanglish Broadway adaptation of the adaptation affirms that in the intervening half-century, nothing important has changed. The most frequently filmed play of all time, *Romeo and Juliet* has been set in Mexico, India, and punk London. It's inspired symphonies by Berlioz and Tchaikovsky, a Prokofiev ballet, a martial arts film starring Jet Li, and at least 24 operas. It's been recognized as the plot source for *Rebel Without a Cause, East of Eden, The Lion King, High School Musical,* and of course, *Shakespeare in Love.* Bruce Springsteen, Dire Straits, Tom Waits, the Supremes, and Lou Reed have woven it into their lyrics. What all these adaptations have in common is a bedrock fascination with the story that begins in love and ends in death.

When Shakespeare introduces Romeo, he's under the sway of eros; more precisely, he's playing the part of a lover under the sway of eros.

Bedazzled and befuddled, he launches himself into poetic transports. "Feather of lead, bright smoke, cold fire," he begins, rambling on until not even his closest friends can repress their amusement. "Dost thou laugh?" the wounded swain asks Benvolio. As anyone knows who's ever provided a (mostly) sympathetic ear to a newly besotted friend, sometimes it's hard not to.

Romeo's lyricism, by the way, is directed not toward Juliet, but Rosaline, whose half-life as the embodiment of feminine perfection expires approximately three seconds after Juliet's appearance. Master of superlatives, Romeo ups the rhetorical ante once he catches a glimpse of Miss Capulet: "Did my heart love till now? Forswear it, sight, For I ne'er saw true beauty till this night." It's both a moment of gentle humor and Shakespeare's reminder—the subtlety of which depends on the individual viewer's past experience and present state of mind—that eros on its own can never be taken at face value. Whether its initial fire will burn steadily or flame out, depends on its connections to philia and agape.

As an experienced aficionado of sensuality, Mercutio serves as the play's theorist of lust. To coax Romeo out of the hiding place where he's retreated to contemplate the wonders of his newfound love, Mercutio commands his friend to appear "in the likeness of a sigh." He "conjures" Romeo by the invocation of "Rosaline's bright eyes, by her high forehead, and her scarlet lip," continuing the inventory until he arrives at her "quivering thigh, And the demesnes that there adjacent lie." Always the erotic realist, Mercutio knows his friend well. After learning that Romeo has transferred his affection to Juliet, Mercutio remains skeptical, describing Romeo's poetic transports as mathematical formulas, "numbers." Romeo's fevered flights extolling Juliet above all women surpass Petrarch's lyrical sonnets to Laura, which established the pattern for Renaissance poets, including Shakespeare. "Now is he for the numbers that Petrarch flowed in," Mercutio marvels. "Laura to his lady was a kitchen wench . . . Dido a dowdy, Cleopatra a gypsy, Helen and Hero hildings and harlots."

Against that backdrop, it was no easy task for Shakespeare to convince his audience to see Romeo's attachment to Juliet as something more than another case of what Mercutio calls "driveling love," the chemical imbalance of a lust-addled clown "who runs lolling up and down to hide his bauble in a hole." The transformation begins when Romeo and Juliet first set eyes on one another at the Capulets' party. In a scene that remains unparalleled in its ability to breathe life into moribund clichés—"some enchanted evening," "love at first sight"—the young lovers weave a perfect sonnet around playful images of eros and agape. Sounding like the Dante of *La Vita Nuova*, Romeo declares his lips "two blushing pilgrims," ready to smooth the "rough touch" of his hand "with a tender kiss." Appropriately suspicious of masculine ardor, however spiritual its trappings, Juliet shifts the focus away from the physical. "Palm to palm is holy palmer's kiss," she replies, teasingly reminding Romeo that true pilgrims use their mouths for prayer. Rising to the occasion, Romeo urges his "dear saint" to "let lips do what hands do." Kissing her, he claims "from my lips to thine my sin is purged." Juliet points out Romeo's difficulty in distinguishing true love from its literary models, telling him "You kiss by th' book." Still, she gives in to the call of eros and grants him a second kiss.

It's a charming game, which only the most jaundiced viewer would try to resist. But as Juliet well knows, the game has a serious undertone. Throughout the play, her challenge will be to convince and remind Romeo that their love is not, in fact, all they need. She's as smitten as he is, but she's not willing to abandon herself to romantic words alone. "Dost thou love me? I know thou wilt say 'Ay,'" she says to him from her balcony. "And I will take thy word. Yet, if thou swear'st, thou mayst prove false. At lovers' perjuries, they say, Jove laughs." Fearful that Romeo's vows will prove as changeable as "th'inconstant moon" by which he swears, she tells him repeatedly not to offer vows or, if he must, to "swear by thy gracious self." Bringing the conversation back to eros, Romeo laments, "O, wilt thou leave me so unsatisfied?" To Juliet's response—"What satisfaction canst thou have tonight?"—there's a simple answer, of course, but not one that's faithful to the true meaning of eros.

As late as the start of Act V, well after the bodies have begun to pile up on stage, Romeo continues to rhapsodize about the blissful future he imagines: "how sweet is love itself possessed, When but love's shadows are so rich in joy!" His declaration that "nothing can be ill if she is well" is patently untrue. Mercutio and Tybalt are dead; Juliet has been cast out of her family; he himself is exiled as a murderer. The longer he stubbornly clings to the illusion that Juliet herself is the whole world, the closer he and his love edge toward tragedy.

Juliet knows better than to share her lover's rosy view of their prospects. Their world instructs women from the cradle forward that eros is at best an untrustworthy ally, at worst an instrument of their subjugation. Her erotic intelligence doesn't require actual sexual experience. It stems from her position as a woman in a society in which women gained their identity from the men they were attached to: first father, then husband, or, if they remained unmarried, a brother or uncle. Juliet knows her father expects to have the final say over whom she will marry. When she resists, he threatens her with the economic consequences of disobedience in terms only slightly less harsh than those Hermia's father used in *Midsummer*: "hang, beg, starve, die in the streets, For, by my soul, I'll ne'er acknowledge thee, Nor what is mine shall never do thee good."

Given the world she lives in, the prospects aren't good for Juliet's attempt to connect the loves. Even her pledge to Romeo that she "will follow thee my lord through the world" can be seen as an exchange of one commodity status for another. No longer her father's possession to be bestowed on whomever he chooses in marriage, she assumes the role of the exalted, but unreal, mistress of Romeo's stylized imagination. In this situation, eros plays a complex and dangerous role. In a truly creative sense, by asserting her erotic self, Juliet is opening a new space for female expression. As the literary scholar Gail Kern Paster observes, "Allowing her husband access to a bedchamber in her father's house,

Juliet leads him into a sexual territory beyond the reach of dramatic representation." That sort of space—cut off from contact with the outside world and its stultifying social conventions—is where eros thrives, at first. In Shakespeare's time and beyond, erotic visionaries from Christopher Marlowe and John Donne to Walt Whitman, D. H. Lawrence and Prince, have invited the objects of their desire to, in Marlowe's words, "come live with me and be my love and we will all the pleasures prove." Speaking the language of the room beyond representation, they call their lovers away to a place where bodies caress the corners of dreams, where candles whisper shadows on the walls, where two people melt into a strange yet wonderful new substance, where the current of agape flows freely from body to soul. A place where a woman is equal to a man.

The problem is that, divorced from the other loves in a society ruled by patriarchal power, that eros-driven vision is little more than another form of Romeo's fevered dream. Hidden in the dark, separated too long from community, eros will shrivel before it can flower into fullness. In *Romeo and Juliet*, the problem is not only that eros is cut off from philia; it's also that agape plays no meaningful role. The primary representative of the institutional church, Friar Laurence, is well-meaning but ineffectual. He doesn't condemn eros, but neither does he seek to guide the young people of his parish toward a full understanding of love. When Romeo shows up early one morning, the friar jokes, "God pardon sin! Wast thou with Rosaline?" His willingness to ignore philia and shirk the responsibilities of agape plays a major role in precipitating the tragedy. Instead of helping Romeo and Juliet obtain their parents' blessing, Friar Laurence says a prayer for Heaven's blessing just before conducting their secret wedding: "So smile the heavens upon this holy act that after hours with sorrow chide us not." Romeo and Juliet's marriage is arguably valid because they have freely consented to it, but their priest should have known that the law alone wouldn't shield them from grief.

Friar Laurence's sin is that he doesn't guide the young lovers out of their secret room into a more public space where their love might be able to breathe freely and flourish. To do so, of course, would mean having to confront the entrenched powers that control his Verona as surely as they do the Vienna of *Measure for Measure*. His punishment, and Juliet and Romeo's misfortune, is that the friar is unable to respond to later events with anything other than incoherent panic and pious clichés. When Paris comes to announce his engagement to Juliet, Friar Laurence has no response. When Juliet awakens in the tomb, unaware of Romeo's death, he shifts the blame to God. "A greater power than we can contradict," he says, "Hath thwarted our intents." Tellingly, his words reduce Juliet to yet another sort of commodity: "I'll dispose of thee among a sisterhood of holy nuns."

When philia and agape fail the lovers, they find themselves slipping into Hell. While the images of Heaven in *Romeo and Juliet* are treated ironically, those of Hell are deadly serious. When the Nurse brings word that Romeo has killed Juliet's cousin Tybalt in a street brawl, the lovers' erotic paradise vanishes in an eye-blink. "What devil art thou that dost torment me thus?" Juliet asks. "This torture should be roared in dismal hell." Romeo responds to his exile by calling the world in which he will be separated from Juliet "purgatory, torture, hell itself." Clinging to his image of Heaven as the place "where Juliet lives," Romeo responds to Friar Laurence's claim that banishment is preferable to exile, by saying "'Banished?' O Friar, the damned use that word in hell." Imagining herself waking up in the tomb, Juliet sketches a scene straight out of Dante's Inferno. She will, she shudders, "madly play with my forefathers' joints, And pluck the mangled Tybalt from his shroud, And, in this rage, with some great kinsman's bone, As with a club, dash out my desp'rate brains."

If, as the enduring fascination with the play suggests, everyone can vividly imagine that Hell and desperately wants to avoid it, the question is: how to keep from falling into it? Like most of Shakespeare's plays, *Romeo and Juliet* offers no map out of the abyss. The characters in the play draw the simplest possible moral from its events: family feuds are bad. None of them seems to be willing to engage the deeper questions that the whole story raises. The young lovers' deaths may or may not bring superficial peace to Verona, but similar tragedies will continue the world over as long as their underlying causes—the commodification of women (and eros); the trivialization of agape; the failure of philia—remain unaddressed.

Her Infinite Variety: *Antony and Cleopatra*

In Cleopatra, Shakespeare came close to expressing—"capturing" is definitely the wrong word—an erotic force that resists all translation and all containment. The "infinite variety" of the Egyptian queen's sexual presence is a matter not of body, but of psyche, imagination, soul. Possessing, and possessed by, an erotic intelligence unsurpassed in life or literature, she overwhelms everyone, especially those who resist her most. When Caesar's man Maecenus declares that political realities require Antony to leave Cleopatra, Antony's ensign Enobarbus says simply, "Never. He will not . . . Other women cloy The appetites they feed but she makes hungry Where most she satisfies." A more sympathetic observer, the great Shakespearean actress Dame Judi Dench, has reflected on the challenges of embodying this limitlessness on stage. Referring to her 1987 performance of Cleopatra, Dench recalled: "I remember a marvellous note that [director] Peter Hall gave me and he said . . . 'don't ever think of coming on for one scene and having to be all of her.' You come on in one scene and show one aspect of her and another scene maybe another aspect of her and so on. By the end of the evening hopefully you will have the whole person, the whole woman."

Antony and Cleopatra brings together all the tensions inherent in Shakespeare's extended meditation on eros: celebration and tragedy; momentary transcendence confronted by intractable reality; sensual Heaven descending into social and spiritual Hell. The play contains a deep, genuine appreciation for eros, but it's tempered by an equally deep awareness of lust's destructive potential. Queen Cleopatra is no more able to change the world than Desdemona, Isabella, or Juliet. Like them, she lives in a world where politics and power shape all relationships, where there's no space in which eros can connect with either philia or agape. Separated from the other loves, eros becomes just another force in the destructive vortex that casts everyone into the abyss.

While Cleopatra occupies the play's dramatic center of gravity, the story unfolds around Antony as he struggles unsuccessfully to balance his erotic and military lives, associated respectively with Egypt and Rome. In the minds of the characters, Rome represents reason, duty, self-control, and order; Egypt stands in for darkness, sensuality, excess, pleasure. Rome is the (simplified) masculine; Egypt the (stereotyped) feminine. Faced with eros, Rome represses, Egypt indulges.

Neither society can conceive of an effective connection between eros and the other loves. Invoked as a rhetorical convenience, the gods of Rome and Egypt recreate human limitations rather than offering a higher, selfless call. Cleopatra is all too obviously human, despite her considerable charms and her assumption of the "habilments of the goddess Isis"; Antony's wife Octavia is the devotee of a spiritually chilly Roman worship. Philia is at times a convenient rhetorical ploy, at other times a weapon. Commenting on the political alliance among Antony, Lepidus and Caesar, which leads to Antony's ill-conceived and sexless marriage to Octavia, Enobarbus dismisses the leaders' vows of friendship. "If you borrow one another's love for the instant," he warns Antony, "you may, when you hear no more words of Pompey, return it again." Unable to accept the fact that true friendship will sometimes speak uncomfortable truths, Antony silences Enobarbus. Philia becomes, as Enobarbus sardonically describes himself, a "considerate stone."

The play's tragedy results from the fact that both Antony and Cleopatra have the potential to transcend the stifling dichotomy between Rome and Egypt, but they never realize it. Antony could live in either world, but neither will accept his connection with the other. Unaware of the dynamic, he vacillates wildly, unable to establish any kind of balance or harmony within himself or his relationships. At the beginning of the play, Antony believes naively that as long as he does his duty as a soldier when summoned, his personal life should be none of Rome's business. "Let Rome in Tiber melt and the wide arch Of the ranged empire fall," he proclaims as he enters with Cleopatra by his side. "Here is my space. Kingdoms are clay." Energized and awed by the array of erotic possibilities before him, he explores the uncharted regions of his being. He tries on his lover's clothes and lends her his sword, feeling no shame or remorse as he notes, "There's not a minute of our lives should stretch Without some pleasure now."

To Roman eyes, Antony's life inside the erotic bubble violates every standard of duty and decency. Antony has become Cleopatra's dupe; his "captain's heart" has become "the bellows and the fan to cool a gypsy's lust." After the inevitable collapse of their alliance, Caesar pays Antony the most damning insult he can imagine. Having betrayed his calling, he "is not more manlike Than Cleopatra, nor the queen of Ptolemy More womanly than he." In today's language: Antony's a pussy. To his compatriots, the decorated officer who dared to explore the world of erotic possibility is nothing but a dupe, who "hath given his empire up to a whore."

Virtually alone among Cleopatra's masculine admirers, Shakespeare sees that image for the patriarchal projection it has always been. His Cleopatra is only distantly related to the emblem of licentiousness who appears in numerous medieval representations of the seven deadly sins: Dante, recall, assigned her to the second circle of Hell among the lustful. Nor does she have much in common with the modern cousins who share her name: Hollywood fantasies, Afrocentric dreams, naked corpses in the necro-pornography of *fin-de-siècle* decadent painting.

For Shakespeare, Cleopatra is a supremely intelligent performer who does everything in her power to redefine her role in the Roman script. When it suits her purposes, she doesn't hesitate to mesmerize her audience with sensual display. But having carefully studied the men she's known, she can also play scenes in "the high Roman fashion." The real challenge Cleopatra poses for audiences and actresses is that she can change roles in the midst of a scene, or sometimes even a sentence.

At times, as when she flees the battle of Actium, she misjudges the situation; every improviser knows the risk of falling flat on stage. But her conversations with her maids make it clear that she knows what she's doing even when she appears to lose control. Drawing on a seemingly inexhaustible well of creative energy, she can become whoever she needs to be while remaining absolutely who she is. Eros can do no more.

As Shakespeare shows us with a profound sadness, that's not enough to keep her out of Hell. When confronted by the crushing reality of Roman power, the best Cleopatra can do is delay the dénouement. After Antony's final military defeat, the only victory she can still claim is to refuse her place in the piece of political theater Caesar is constructing to show that he has vanquished Egypt and eros: parading her in public as a conquered queen. She knows better than to trust his offer of friendship and pledge of honorable treatment. "He words me girls, he words me, that I should not be noble to myself," she tells her serving maidens. Turning her mind toward death, and claiming the Roman virtues of nobility and fortitude for herself, she describes the scene in which she refuses to act: "The quick comedians Extemporally will stage us and present Our Alexandrian revels. Antony shall be brought drunken forth, and I shall see Some squeaking Cleopatra boy my greatness I' th' posture of a whore." Those ironic lines underscore the fact that for Cleopatra, there is no escape in life or on the stage. She delivers those lines near the end of a play performed in London, Shakespeare's world's equivalent of imperial Rome. The "revels" have opened with a drunken Antony being led forth; the Cleopatra speaking the lines *was* played by a boy.

The only way for Cleopatra to re-assert control over her life is to stage her own death. Playing the Roman role with greater conviction and awareness than anyone in Caesar's entourage, she readies herself for the serpent's bite: "My resolution's placed, and I have nothing Of woman in me. Now from head to foot I am marble-constant. Now the fleeting moon No planet is of mine." Unable to connect eros with the other loves, the supreme embodiment of sensual vitality submits herself to death.

In a literal but little-noted manner, Shakespeare places Antony and Cleopatra's tragedy under the sign of Eros—according to some classical sources, the son of Aphrodite (the goddess of love) and Ares (god of war). Never averse to straining credibility to make a point, the playwright bestowed the name of Eros on the servant who attends Antony during the final hours of his life. Beginning at the point when it becomes clear that the lovers will not be able to escape their doom, Antony calls out Eros's name almost twenty times, providing a ghostly Greek chorus as everything falls apart. Antony pleads with Eros to kill him, but his servant refuses, instead stabbing himself. Chastened, Antony takes up the sword himself. "But I will be a bridegroom in my death and run into 't As to a lover's bed. Come then, and, Eros, Thy master dies thy scholar." The irony is crushing. In Caesar's friendless, godless, loveless world, the spirit of life has become the servant of death. Eros is nothing but an empty echo as Shakespeare leaves us in Hell.

Jane Austen

CHAPTER THREE

"Jane Austen's Guide to the Feminist Purgatory, or, 'He (or sometimes She) Seemed Just Fine Until….'"

Like the sisters in *Pride and Prejudice*, each of the five women at the center of Karen Joy Fowler's novel *The Jane Austen Book Club* has her own sense of what it means to love. As each gazes into Austen's finely polished mirrors, she sees an image of the writer that matches her needs: benevolent comic genius, romantic idealist, keen-witted satirist, tragic artist cut off in her prime. Acutely aware of Austen's insight into "the impact of financial need on the intimate lives of women," a 30-year-old lesbian feminist offers the most trenchant insight: "If she'd worked in a bookstore, Allegra would have shelved Austen in the horror section."

It's a joke and it isn't. However genteel the surface of their lives, Austen's heroines face threats as harrowing as the blade-wielding maniacs, soul-sucking aliens, and seductive vampires who fill the pages of Edgar Allan Poe, Stephen King, and Anne Rice. It was only a matter of time until the metaphor took literal shape in *Pride and Prejudice and Zombies* and *Sense and Sensibility and Sea Monsters*. As in the macabre classics and their pop culture clones, erotic phantoms haunt the margins of Austen's novels, flickering just beyond the range of vision, enticing, confusing, and sometimes paralyzing those who deny their reality. Wandering a deceptively normal landscape populated mostly by the unseeing, Austen's heroines repeatedly turn to philia for sustenance in a society that subordinates both agape and eros to economic interests. Aware of the twin traps of commodification and repression, they imagine love stories in which connections based on humor, mutual respect, and shared values emerge as the real-world ideal for women who want to live the fullest possible lives before and after marriage.

Despite the destructive forces surrounding them, Austen's heroines aren't living in Hell. As a nineteenth-century Anglican, Austen wouldn't have used the term Purgatory, but Dante would recognize the confused couples of *Pride and Prejudice*, *Emma*, and *Mansfield Park* as close relatives of the souls ascending the terraces in the second book of the *Divine Comedy*. Like Dante's penitents, Austen's characters are engaged in a process of intellectual and spiritual growth that inevitably causes them pain, but holds out the hope of lasting rewards. Confronting their failings and those of the people around them, they gradually learn how to support one another as they face problems that remain depressingly recognizable in the twenty-first-century world of Internet dating, office affairs, pick-up bars, and church-sponsored Christian singles groups. Psychological descendants of the Bennet sisters and Emma Woodhouse, we confuse attractive exteriors with real worth, indulge in rumors and gossip, factor finance into our assessment of potential lovers, delude ourselves about our motives. In our more lucid moments, we sense there's a better way and know we can't find it alone.

Which is why, even for those of us who don't know a curricle from a quadrille, Austen remains a beacon in the socio-sexual darkness. You could stock a medium-sized library with adaptations, updates, and sequels to her novels. Inspired by *Pride and Prejudice* and *Sense and Sensibility*, literarily-inclined Janeites (a term coined in the 1890s) have contemplated the tensions between *Illusion and Ignorance*, *Affinity and Affection*, *Drive and Determination*, and—alliteration be d****d—*Fate and Consequences*. The hero of *Pride and Prejudice* has received loving (and not infrequently lascivious) attention in *Mr. Darcy, The Other Mr.*

Darcy, Darcy's Passion, Darcy's Temptation, Loving Mr. Darcy, Waiting for Mr. Darcy, Seducing Mr. Darcy, and, to return to an earlier theme, *Mr. Darcy, Vampire* and *Vampire Darcy's Desire*. A shelf or two would be set aside for sagas of women who shape their lives according to lessons they attribute to the sage of Hampshire, among them *Confessions of A Jane Austen Addict, What Would Jane Austen Do, Jane Austen Ruined My Life*, and of course *The Jane Austen Book Club*.

Funds to purchase the collection could be raised via the Jane Austen Film Festival. Wandering far afield from the familiar countryside of the relatively faithful and hugely popular BBC adaptations of the collected works, her heroines have found themselves living in the Beverly Hills of *Clueless*, the Amritsar of the Bollywood vehicle *Bride and Prejudice*, the London of *Bridget Jones' Diary* and *Lost in Austen*, and the inner cities of the hip-hop musical *Emma* and the Spanglish *Sense and Sensibilidad*. Even when the titles remain the same, the heroines change clothes and character to reflect the fashions and values of the moment. Ads for the 1940 movie version of *Pride and Prejudice* starring Laurence Olivier and Greer Garson feature a line of primly hopeful sisters chirping "We want a husband," while the poster for the 2005 remake foregrounds a disheveled Keira Knightley pursued by a distinctly Byronesque Matthew Macfadyen who would have horrified the original Mr. Darcy. The American version of the 2005 film ends with Knightley and Macfadyen in an erotic clinch, an addition that one English movie executive likened to the French practice of adding sugar to Champagne destined for American palates. The British release ends in defensibly Austenian fashion, with Mr. Bennet commenting wryly: "If any young men come for Mary or Kitty, send them in, for I am quite at leisure."

Even the most trendy and transient adaptations have the virtue of directing Janeites, fledgling and experienced, back to their sources. Austen's novels model the process of growth they describe, using grace, wit, and intelligence to coax beauty out of unpromising material, helping us think, and live, through the complexities of love. Living in an officially Christian society where agape is too often confused with respectability,

Austen's heroines rely on each other's support in a world where money consistently trumps ideals; and where being "reasonable"—accommodating to patriarchy, inside and outside the church—is the highest value. They fantasize about flawed men, come to a sometimes-bitter understanding of their status as objects in a sexual marketplace, and weigh the trade-offs between financial security, family obligation, and erotic desire. Two centuries after the publication of *Pride and Prejudice*, only the most fortunate, or oblivious, women bother to pretend we're living in a different world. Now, as then, hardly anyone's pretty or rich enough to do as she pleases—and anyway, Austen reminds us, doing as we please isn't the goal. Her storylines resonate with (straight) grown-up women who've decided to focus on their relationships with their girlfriends instead of waiting around for so-called Mr. Right; with younger women who want to live their lives in partnership with, rather than in the shadow of, a man; and with any woman who's been dumped by a friend for a guy—or done the dumping and repented of it after he's gone his way. Often we learn the hard way, but as Austen's heroines know, learning and growing together is what our journey is about.

Austen's Purgatory

For Austen, growth was personal, but it always happened in community, and that's one of the most important lessons she has to teach her twenty-first-century sisters and brothers. If we look through her sharp eyes and follow her dry wit where it leads us, we see that our dreams are often individualistic, while those of her heroines always take others into account. "Follow your bliss" would have been an incomprehensible piece of advice in Austen's world, where mutual aid and support thrive in the face of stultifying social conventions. Her heroines have friends and sisters they're loath to leave behind for marriage, and they're constantly figuring out their lives together. Like the souls arriving in Dante's Purgatory, these women are learning to sing with one voice, or at least in a homemade harmony, and along the way they're finding out just how complicated it is to make music together. But even their struggle has its joys, as they weave a network of relationships among themselves and their male and female neighbors.

Austen envisioned those networks primarily in terms of philia; she had a complicated relationship with agape, which was inseparable from the institutional and theological traditions of Anglicanism. The daughter and sister of parsons, baptized when she was one day old, Austen was a faithful member of the Church of England. As her biographer Irene Collins has noted, she wrote prayers modeled on the Book of Common Prayer for family services; and her library included devotional reading like *A Companion to the Altar*, a guide to preparing to receive Communion. Even though she never earned enough from her writing to support herself, she devoted about a quarter of her income to pew rents and charity. But she was also aware of the ways in which the Church's implication in networks of economic and political power compromised its ability to guide its members toward lives that honored both agape and eros.

In the institutional context of Austen's England, anyone—especially a woman—who expressed a desire to connect their erotic and spiritual lives might as well have been speaking in tongues, without an interpreter. Hypocrisy and commodification were woven into the fabric of everyday life, especially but not exclusively in regard to eros. In the church, as in drawing rooms, legal chambers, and the dining halls of Oxford and Cambridge, women's roles were tightly circumscribed. Agape was present in the Church of England's theology, liturgy, and charitable works, but when conflicts with economic interests arose, compassion rarely carried the day. While Austen respected dedicated clergymen, she had seen how many young men became priests simply because parishes, revealingly referred to as "livings," represented their best economic option. Religious positions, like military commissions and government posts, were typically conferred by benefactors, often related to the recipient by blood or marriage. Eldest sons were expected to inherit and manage family estates; younger brothers to "take orders"—the double meaning is suggestive—with little regard for whether or not they felt a religious calling. As was so often the case for their marriageable sisters, duty trumped desire.

Similarly, the Church of England's commitment to embodying a "middle way" between Catholic and Protestant practices and beliefs, while providing much-needed social stability after a period of religious conflict, provided Austen with a thinner theological vocabulary than those available to Dante and Shakespeare. The Protestant Reformation had vehemently repudiated the dogma of Purgatory, the Church of England denouncing it as "a fond thing, vainly invented, and grounded upon no warranty of Scripture, but rather repugnant to the Word of God." It's not surprising that Austen never uses the term. Nonetheless, the issues Dante and Shakespeare associated with Purgatory were very much in her mind, and as central to her world as they were to fourteenth-century Florence or sixteenth-century London: realizing our mistakes and failings, seeking forgiveness, and finding a better path with the help of honest, loving friends. Austen did not have to believe in Purgatory as a "real" place or state of being to be deeply conscious of the link between repentance and spiritual growth, or to respond to the *Companion to the Altar*'s call to practice examination of conscience, so that "henceforward no secret sin may lie undiscovered and corrupt the soul."

Adapting the institutional and theological resources at her disposal, Austen placed philia at the center of her vision. Like the souls in Dante's Purgatory, Austen's characters thirst for a fuller experience of love and they struggle to form fragile communities with others who share that desire. Forming family-centered networks of friends and neighbors, Austen's characters work together to learn the practice of love through trial and error, sustaining and encouraging each other in the hope of ultimately being healed. Each person's actions matter to everyone; characters—and readers—can reflect on the choices they've made and share hard-earned wisdom. No one who stretches out a hand is left to suffer alone. In comparison with Dante, the spiritual odysseys of Austen's characters take place on a circumscribed stage: she famously (although, possibly, ironically) described her own work to her nephew James as "the little bit (two Inches wide) of Ivory on which I work with so fine a brush." Readers willing to follow Austen where she leads, however, can learn as much about human life and hope as Dante did when Virgil guided him out of the Inferno's depths to the threshold of Paradise.

In his exploration of moral theory, *After Virtue*, philosopher Alisdair MacIntyre offers a provocative reflection on the similarity between Austen and Dante: "Austen writes comedy rather than tragedy for the same reason that Dante did," MacIntyre writes, "she is a Christian and she sees the telos of human life implicit in its everyday form." In other words, they both know that our means—how we live every day—has to reflect our end—what kind of person we want to be at the end of those days. MacIntyre's emphasis on what Austen and Dante have in common is apt, but there are two important differences between the two writers' visions of Purgatory. First, and most simply: the souls in the Divine Comedy are dead. Those who've arrived in Purgatory know they'll make it to Paradise eventually. That knowledge gives them a joyous confidence that Austen's characters (like the living Dante in the poem) can't fully share. They're still alive, with plenty of time to put their souls in jeopardy, so they can't be certain of their fate. Second, women lived in very different social conditions in Dante's and Austen's worlds. Without romanticizing fourteenth-century Florence as a feminist Paradise, it's fair to say Austen's heroines confront social conventions that offer them even less opportunity than Beatrice and her companions to fully express eros. Lacking the freedom that is the wellspring of all loves, especially eros and agape, they turn to philia. For Austen, however, philia alone can't unite the loves, in part because it's implicated in networks of exchange; we take care of our family and friends with the assumption they'll do the same for us when we need it. As rich and necessary as philia is to human life, eros and agape are even more generous, and, in their true forms can only be offered freely. Nonetheless, however flawed and fumbling as Austen's heroines may be, however resistant the patriarchal society in which they live, they refuse to surrender their *hope* of

Paradise—and that's a great source of Austen's appeal. She offers a view of real women, operating within recognizable constraints, who never stop hoping and working for a life that harmonizes love in all its forms.

And now a few words from the not particularly loyal opposition.

The View from the Patriarchy

At some point in every discussion of Jane Austen, custom dictates that the stage be yielded to Mark Twain. "Any library is a good library that does not contain a volume by Jane Austen," cracked America's beloved, crusty, and more than slightly misanthropic, humorist, "Even if it contains no other book." "Every time I read *Pride and Prejudice*," he elaborated in a letter to a friend, "I want to dig her up and beat her over the skull with her own shin-bone." Resisting the temptation to speculate on why Twain would have subjected himself to such torment more than once, we'll move through the honor roll of those who have echoed his complaint: film director Ang Lee, who claimed he hadn't bothered to read Austen before directing *Sense and Sensibility*; the influential literary critic George Sampson, editor of *The Cambridge History of English Literature*, who dismissed her novels as feminine fantasies fixated on the "make-believe mating of dolls"; D. H. Lawrence, who labeled her an "old maid" typifying all that is "English in the bad, mean, snobbish sense of the word"; and socialist novelist H. G. Wells who called her a "lovely butterfly" with "no guts at all."

We hope our gentle readers will not be too terribly shocked to learn that the vast majority of those who have applauded such positions are, to use the technical term, *boys*. Those in search of dissenting masculine opinions are directed to Steve Chandler and Terrence Hill's amusingly insightful *Two Guys Read Jane Austen* and the nineteen male-authored chapters in *A Truth Universally Acknowledged: 33 Great Writers on Why We Read Jane Austen*. Leaving Mr. Clemens and his associates to the pleasures of shin-bone beating and the revised edition of *The Joy of Hunting*, we now return to the business at hand.

Aunt Jane Unbound

If Austen is a butterfly, she belongs to the same phylum as Muhammad Ali. Floating gracefully but possessed of a wicked sting, Austen crafted a deceptively powerful prose capable of reducing her antagonists to a state of anaphylactic shock. No writer, Dante or Shakespeare included, has seen more deeply into the way social conventions and entrenched thought patterns—such as those that confuse reserve with weakness—can make it impossible for *anyone*, male or female, to harmonize the three loves. Drawing on a complex and intensely personal sense of eros and refusing to accept social veneer as truth, Austen devoted her razor-sharp intelligence to resisting the forces of repression and commodification that continue to haunt us today.

And yet the image persists of the nineteenth century's finest satirist as a sexually frustrated old maid whose novels served as, in the words of Virginia Woolf's husband Leonard, "compensation daydreams for her failure in real life." Pause a moment to visualize her. The picture that comes to mind almost certainly has little to do with the single likeness made during Austen's lifetime: a sketch by her sister showing a young woman in a simple dress and plain bonnet, arms folded in a position expressing firmness, an ironic twist to her lips. Not a touch of finery or spinsterish regret. Part of a concerted effort by Austen's family to sanitize (and cash in on) her image, the transformation into "Dear Aunt Jane" began after Austen's death when her nephew James commissioned a portrait to accompany his *Memoir*, which included the first published selection of her correspondence. Adding a demure smile along with ruffles on her bonnet and neckline, the new and improved portrait cast a veil of moon-dust over the actual woman. It was the visual equivalent of James' editorial decision to remove from his aunt's letters all references to politics and the human body, as well as her frequently caustic, and distinctly unladylike, observations on human frailty. Working from the published image rather than the original, later artists added a proliferation of ringlets, ruffles, and billows to Austen's hair and clothing, separated her arms, hung a cross around her neck, sprinkled her with rosebuds, and placed a wedding ring on her left hand, presumably as recompense for maidenly suffering.

A slightly less repressed but no less distorted Austen takes center stage in the charmingly speculative movie *Becoming Jane*, the Janeite equivalent of *Shakespeare in Love*. Based on Austen's "attachment"—to use her era's term—to Irish law student Tom Lefroy, the adaptation of Jon Spence's biography subordinates Austen's fierce commitment to her art to a warmed-over romantic cliché. The outline of events is simple: after a mutual flirtation that many, including Austen, expected would lead to an engagement, Lefroy backed off, probably because of financial obligations to his large family. While Austen was clearly disappointed, she did not spend the rest of her life pining away. Far from being an embittered spinster—twice she turned down economically advantageous marriage proposals—she *chose* to devote herself to the books that justify novelist Margaret Drabble's claim that "There would be more genuine rejoicing at the discovery of a complete new novel by Jane Austen than any other literary discovery, short of a new major play by Shakespeare."

The power of her novels flows not from anodyne wish fulfillment or saccharine sentimentality, but from her improvisational genius and her clarity about the constraints within which her heroines live. Austen knew full well that her own experience was just one example of women's struggles to live out their deepest desires, and she documented that struggle with a deep truthfulness that appears more often in stories than in what we call real life. From their early teens on, Austen's women are assigned roles based on their value as marriageable objects. Understandably concerned with assuring their daughters' financial security in a society where middle-class respectability could be all too easily lost, families like those of her characters sought alliances that would increase their fortune or social standing. Austen knew from personal experience how strong the pressure to accept a "good offer" was, given women's short shelf life as erotic merchandise. Resisting that pressure with wily determination, the real Jane Austen (as distinct from the wistful wallflower who encounters her long-ago suitor in the fictional final scene of *Becoming Jane*) stated the take-home message in her response to the engagement of a niece who had shown signs of writing talent. "Oh! What a loss it will be, when you are married. I shall hate you when your delicious play of Mind is all settled down into conjugal & maternal affections." Even allowing for playful overstatement, that comment tells a central truth of Austen's day: it was almost impossible to imagine a woman channeling eros into both her marriage and her art.

In the absence of obvious alternatives, it's not surprising that many women, motivated by fear, obedience, or simple awareness of their limited options, would accept their assigned roles, in effect dismissing eros from their lives. The situation was complicated by the fact that, as Austen knew, an eros-filled marriage held significant risks. In the absence of effective contraception, sexual desire increased the likelihood of frequent pregnancy, which carried real dangers. It was not unusual for women of her era to give birth to two children every three years for a decade or more. Upon hearing of a young relative's pregnancy, Austen wrote to a friend, "Poor animal, she will be worn out before she is thirty!"

Although there were no easy solutions to these dilemmas—there still aren't—Austen's heroines are shielded from the extremes that cast many of Shakespeare's lovers into Hell. No one threatens her young women that they will starve, beg, or die in the streets if they don't follow their father's wishes. The occasional character who elopes is eventually re-incorporated into her family, her foolishness fortifying her sisters' resolve not to disappoint their father and break their mother's heart. Disruptions are reintegrated into the social fabric rather than spiraling out of control; the novels end not with death, but with the promise of marriage. But like Shakespeare who ended *As You Like It* with a quartet of betrothals, Austen knew that happy endings were conventional: responses to the audience's desires that reflect back on the nature of those desires. Celebrated in a world of cross-purposes and confusion, the weddings aren't destinations, but points of departure for a journey that continues in the lives of her readers. Her novels take their real meaning when we respond to them not by asking, "What would Jane do?" but by accepting their challenge to imagine and create a world in which philia provides the foundation for mending the broken connections among the three loves.

FAMILY, FRIENDS—AND LOVERS?: *PRIDE AND PREJUDICE*

Pride and Prejudice poses the question of the relationship between philia and eros in a society where both are dependent variables in complex equations. From the opening paragraphs, Austen emphasizes the economic constraints on eros: "a single man in possession of a good fortune," she writes with humor and brutal realism, is universally understood by the rural middle class to be "the rightful property of some one or other of their daughters." In that society, even young girls quickly learn the math. Born into a family lacking the economic resources that give women a significant say in their marital destinies, some of the Bennet sisters calculate well, others poorly, but none can afford not to count costs. Their situation isn't hopeless, but it is difficult, sometimes agonizing, and not even Elizabeth and Jane's arrival at successful solutions to the "suitor problem" changes the nature of the game.

For the mothers and fathers in Austen's novels, their daughters' potential suitors might as well have their incomes tattooed on their foreheads. Very shortly after Mr. Bingley's arrival in their neighborhood, Mrs. Bennet knows he has "four or five thousand a year," and Mr. Darcy's arrival is accompanied by the news that his annual income is ten thousand pounds, an unthinkably—but enticingly—large sum to the local matrons. Mrs. Bennet's fixation on men's financial "worth" stems more from need than from greed. Young women of her class aren't equipped to make a living; she has five daughters, and no sons to provide a home for any left unmarried. Since women can't inherit the family home, it will pass to a cousin, Mr. Collins, upon their father's death. If Mr. Bennet dies before his daughters are married, they and their mother will be "destitute enough," left with the impossible challenge of living on the two hundred pounds a year his small savings earn. Mrs. Bennet doesn't hesitate to remind Elizabeth of that fact, when the young woman turns down Mr. Collins's marriage proposal. "Miss Lizzy, if you take it into your head to go on refusing every offer of marriage in this way, you will never get a husband at all," she scolds, "and I am sure I do not know who is to maintain you when your father is dead.—*I shall not be able to keep you*—and so I warn you." Mr. Bennet, for his part, despises Mr. Collins and warns his daughter humorously that he will never see her again if she accepts the proposal—but as a man, Mr. Bennet has the luxury of knowing that his home is his own as long as he lives.

Refusing to blind herself to economic reality or to give up on passion, Elizabeth seeks the best solution their society can imagine to the problem of eros: a good marriage in which networks of family and friendship surround lovers united by bonds of love, intelligence and respect. Philia plays a pivotal role in that ideal vision. It's crucial that a woman be able to imagine her suitor not only as a friend and lover for life, but also as a faithful brother and son to add to the family.

Still, Austen knows eros *is* real. While she adheres to the social and literary conventions forbidding direct reference to physical desire, *Pride and Prejudice* abounds in sexual energy, veiling its fierce erotic intelligence in references to characters' "bewitching" qualities and the sometimes feverish "admiration" they feel in one another's presence. The first indication of Darcy's attraction to Elizabeth takes place after she asserts her independence by walking alone to Netherfield upon hearing of her sister Jane's illness. When she arrives, her complexion is flushed, her "face glowing" and, Austen writes with a sly glance at Darcy, "she attracted him more than he liked."

As the two begin to overrule their reservations about each other's suitability, eros moves into the foreground. A tall, handsome hero who could have stepped off the pages of a Harlequin romance, Darcy finds himself once again "overflowing with admiration" while Elizabeth "lay awake two whole hours" trying to come to terms with feelings that, in her world, travel under assumed names. One of the crucial moments in

Pride and Prejudice occurs when she forces herself to acknowledge, and take responsibility for, her erotic power: "Such a change in a man of so much pride, excited not only astonishment but gratitude—for to love, ardent love, it must be attributed; and as such its impression on her was of a sort to be encouraged, as by no means unpleasing, though it could not be exactly defined. She respected, she esteemed, she was grateful to him, she felt a real interest in his welfare; and she only wanted to know how far she wished that welfare to depend upon herself, and how far it would be for the happiness of both that she should employ the power, which her fancy told her she still possessed, of bringing on the renewal of his addresses."

Our goal here is not to swell the ranks of the enthusiasts who have conjured up evidence of lesbianism, masturbation, and sadomasochism in Austen's novels—for the harrowing, hallucinatory and not infrequently hilarious details see *Pride and Promiscuity: The Lost Sex Scenes of Jane Austen*—but to insist that she considers the ability to accept and express erotic awareness fundamental to psychological and social health. The novel Austen actually wrote focuses on the more realistic problems of indulging or repressing eros. The near-disastrous elopement of the youngest Bennet sister, Lydia, with the dashing but unscrupulous Captain Wickham demonstrates what can happen when a woman gives herself up to romantic fantasy. A compendium of melodramatic clichés enlivened by Austen's ironic tone, Lydia's narrow escape from degradation serves to remind her sisters, and readers, of the potential dangers of eros. Her sister Mary is her opposite; if Lydia is insufficiently cautious, Mary is overly so. Shaking her head in disapproval of her sister's unthinking pursuit of eros, Mary articulates a working theory of repression. "Unhappy as the event may be for Lydia," she sermonizes, "we may draw from it this useful lesson; that loss of virtue in a female is irretrievable—that one false step involves her in endless ruin—that her reputation is no less brittle than it is beautiful—and that she cannot be too much guarded in her behavior towards the undeserving of the other sex."

The story of Elizabeth's friend Charlotte Lucas sounds a cautionary note of a more complex sort. An intelligent and sympathetic woman who deserves love and happiness, Charlotte accepts her economically determined "fate," settling for an arid marriage to the clergyman Mr. Collins, the Bennet cousin and heir whose proposal Elizabeth previously turned down. Neither sensible nor attractive—Austen goes out of her way to identify him as a very bad dancer—Collins views his clerical duties as a bothersome distraction from his fawning devotion to his rich relative, Lady Catherine de Bourgh. In accepting his hand, Charlotte forgoes both eros and agape and is forced to live far from her beloved friends. At the age of twenty-seven (well into spinsterhood for her time), with no other offers on the table, she's prepared to make the loveless bargain, telling a shocked Elizabeth, "I am not romantic you know. I never was. I ask only a comfortable home; and considering Mr. Collins's character, connections, and situation in life, I am convinced that my chance of happiness with him is as fair, as most people can boast on entering the married state." Few of us would make such a stark statement anymore, but given women's persistent economic disadvantages, a man's job, house, and career prospects continue to figure, often without honest acknowledgment, into many marital negotiations.

Elizabeth's own rejection of Mr. Collins and her refusal of Darcy's initial proposal show how unwilling she is either to accept a marriage lacking in eros, or to be swept away by a handsome face, however well-situated the man who wears it. Where Charlotte sizes up her own chances with a dismal, if realistic, eye, Elizabeth has too much confidence in her ironic intelligence. She interprets Darcy's every move in ways that question his sincerity, only lowering her defenses against his erotic appeal when she realizes how central philia is to his character. The turning point comes when, encountering him accidentally on his own estate, she sees his generous love for his younger sister and the reciprocal affection shown by his staff. "What praise more valuable than the praise of an intelligent servant?" she reflects. "As a brother, a landlord, a master, she considered how many people's happiness were in his guardianship!—How much of pleasure or pain it was in his power to bestow!—How much of good or evil must be done by him!" As the reserved lovers inch closer to one another, Darcy reveals a degree of self-awareness that allows Elizabeth to let go of her prejudice against what she had thought was his prideful bearing, and start to see him in a new light. Being an only son, he reflects, "almost taught me to be selfish and overbearing, to care for none beyond my own family circle, to think meanly of all the rest of the world, to *wish* at least to think meanly of their sense and worth compared with my own." Improvising a way through the quirks of their own characters as well as their society's constraints, Elizabeth and Darcy commit themselves to a marriage that will embed their erotic connection in circles of philia.

The Bennet sisters' struggles to join those two loves, to marry men who are their friends and who can be incorporated into their families, are all too familiar today. The economic pressures on single women may have diminished, but they haven't vanished. Women's shelf life in what's still called "the market" remains much shorter than men's, whose ability to pair off with much younger partners contributes to their higher rates of remarriage after divorce or the death of a spouse. In the years since the emergence of the "*Playboy* philosophy" that cloaked hedonistic self-indulgence in the guise of erotic liberation, significant numbers of men have granted themselves a freedom to abandon their families that would have horrified Austen's characters, male and female. Single mothers—and the single fathers who are less numerous, but who face challenges of their own—know how important it is to be able to rely on family and friends, and they know how hard it still can be to connect eros to a web of philia.

That difficulty points to a deeper tension in Austen's work. While *Pride and Prejudice* asserts a notion of philia that is both broad and deep, Austen senses that philia alone is not sufficient to provide a convincing answer to all of the questions the novel raises. Even the most generous acts are entangled in the web of economic exchange. Darcy's payment of the dowry Lydia needs in order to avoid being abandoned—"ruined" in the language of the time—is without question grounded in philia, and his kindness convinces Elizabeth of his character. But it also places her at a disadvantage inherent in the economic system. She finds it "painful, exceedingly painful" to know that she and her family "were under obligations to a person who could never receive a return" because of the difference in their wealth. In the end, Darcy does receive something of a return, in the form of Elizabeth herself, and his incorporation into the family he has provided for. However deep and sincere their love, it can never be entirely free. Neither of the lovers can simply will that tension away. In the absence of an explicit notion of agape, in a world where generous compassion can be in short supply, Darcy's acts provide a model, but not a foundation for resolving the tension between the loves. Austen would return to those problems in the story of Fanny Price.

The Cross and the Chain: Mansfield Park

The quest to balance the three loves lies at the heart of *Mansfield Park*, Austen's most undervalued novel and the one in which she deals most directly with the church. Preparing for a ball in her honor, the heroine, Fanny Price, faces a decision about how to wear an amber cross, a gift from her beloved brother William and the most powerful symbol of agape in Austen's fiction. Under social pressure to hang it from an ornate necklace given to her as part of a seduction scheme launched by the rake Henry Crawford, Fanny strongly prefers the simple gold chain she received from Edmund, a dear friend and the object of her unspoken love. The economically prudent choice would be to accept Henry's advances, but her heart, mind and soul resist. The successful resolution of Fanny's dilemma—the cross won't fit onto the thick necklace, so she threads it onto the thin chain—gives rise to Austen's most moving celebration of the harmony of the three loves. "With delightful feelings," Austen writes, Fanny "joined the chain and the cross, those memorials of the two most beloved of her heart, those dearest tokens so formed for each other by every thing real and imaginary—and put them around her neck." Seeing and feeling "how full of William and Edmund they were, she was able, without an effort, to resolve on wearing Miss Crawford's necklace too." The three gifts signify harmony among agape, eros, and philia, providing her with the strength she needs to resist the pressures she'll face as an erotic commodity at the ball and beyond.

The cross and the chain provide points of reference both for Fanny's struggle to balance the three loves and for Austen's skewering of Christian hypocrites, the most obvious, but not the most important, religious theme of *Mansfield Park*. Fanny's aunt, Mrs. Norris, is a clergyman's wife who might be expected to keep a place at her table and a bed in her house for travelers or the needy, but instead she's one of the least hospitable and most judgmental characters in all of fiction. Thomas's sister Mary Crawford, a cynical young woman whose beauty mesmerizes Edmund, holds a contempt for the church that has just enough basis in reality to ring true to readers, then and now. Dismissing the possibility of a genuine vocation, Mary informs Edmund that it is "indolence and love of ease—a want of laudable ambition, of taste for good company, or of inclination to take the trouble of being agreeable, which make men Clergymen." The demands on the rector, or head of a parish, are simply to "read the newspaper, watch the weather, and quarrel with his wife. His curate does all the work, and the business of his own life is to dine." Austen knew better than to offer a blanket denial; many priests did treat their livings in a cavalier fashion, delivering formulaic sermons and maintaining their primary residence in fashionable locales remote from their rural parishes. But she also knew that wasn't the whole story. Edmund answers Mary calmly: "There are such Clergymen, no doubt, but I think they are not so common as to justify Miss Crawford in esteeming it their general character." His acts respond more clearly than his words; his vocation is genuine and he intends to live in his beloved parish where he grew up and his family remains.

Austen introduces the issue of clerical irresponsibility into *Mansfield Park* in part to clear the way for the novel's most important engagement with religion: its portrait of people of genuine faith seeking to live out all the loves in community. The story revolves around Fanny Price, whose mother's elopement, and subsequent struggle to support nine children, offer ample evidence of the dangers inherent in the unreflective pursuit of eros. At the age of ten, Fanny is sent to live at the country estate of her mother's sister and her husband Sir Thomas Bertram, a minor nobleman. The distinctions between Fanny and the Bertram children—two daughters and two sons—give the story its erotic tension. They grow up together, but are never treated as siblings, so that when the eighteen-year-old Fanny develops erotic feelings for her older cousin Edmund, her love is clearly not incestuous. Sadly for Fanny, Edmund sees her only as a dear friend. Infatuated with the rich but spiritually empty Mary Crawford, Edmund spends most of the novel struggling to reconcile his genuine calling to the priesthood with his confused and (unconsciously) commodified erotic desires.

In a society where the reigning assumption is that eros must be bought, Edmund won't and Fanny can't. She's out of place in the local marriage market: beyond the reach of men of her parents' class because of her association with the Bertrams, but with no dowry or social standing to offer a wealthy husband. When Mary Crawford's brother Henry suddenly proposes to Fanny, no one can understand why she refuses. She tells her uncle simply, "I cannot like him, Sir, well enough to marry him." Fanny believes it would be "unpardonable" and "wicked" "to marry without affection." To her uncle, she's being "wilful and perverse" by refusing to enter into a marriage that could benefit her brothers and sisters, for the sake of what he calls "a young, heated fancy." Henry doesn't give up. Taking a leaf from the young Dante's *La Vita Nuova*, he drafts agape into the service of eros, using spiritual language as a tool of seduction. Seeking to win Fanny over by first engaging Edmund in a serious discussion of the Book of Common Prayer, he woos her in the language of worship. "You have qualities which I had not before supposed to exist in such a degree in any human creature," he effuses, "you have some touches of the angel in you, beyond what—not merely beyond what one sees, because one never sees anything like it—

but beyond what one fancies might be." Henry acknowledges that, as a mere mortal, he can never be Fanny's spiritual equal. What he asks is the opportunity to show that he's the man "who sees and worships your merit the strongest, who loves you most devotedly."

Like Beatrice before her, Fanny has no interest in being seen as an angel instead of the flesh-and-blood woman she is, and she has even more reason than Beatrice to be suspicious of her suitor's lofty compliments. Just a few weeks earlier, Henry had been involved in a feverish love triangle with Edmund's sisters Maria and Julia. Taking advantage of Sir Thomas's absence on business and bored by the long winter in the countryside, the young people of the neighborhood plan to put on a play, "Lover's Vow." The rehearsals rapidly devolve into a series of dalliances and jealousies, Austen's equivalent of a bedroom farce. As in Shakespeare's comedies, the farce points to serious conflicts that threaten to rip the community to shreds. Edmund and Mary are assigned the roles of a couple in love. Too shy to say her lines for the first time to Edmund, Mary approaches Fanny for help rehearsing; they've worked through half a scene when Edmund arrives in Fanny's sitting room, also seeking her aid. Fanny's pleasure at seeing Edmund turns to misery as he and Mary begin to rehearse together, with Fanny acting as chaperone and prompter. Her emotional state reflects her impossible position: "To prompt them must be enough for her; and it was sometimes *more* than enough," as she becomes more and more miserable. At one point, when, "agitated by the increasing spirit of Edmund's manner," Fanny "closed the page and turned away exactly as he wanted help," her actions are interpreted as fatigue, and she is "thanked and pitied" by the two who don't realize they're tormenting her.

The erotic undercurrent runs closer to the surface in another wing of the house, where Maria and Thomas rehearse their lovers' parts every chance they get. Their flirtation drives a wedge between the two Bertram sisters, leaving Julia to suffer angrily. The sisters had been "very good friends while their interests were the same," but, cast in the roles of erotic competitors, they desert philia. Lacking a conscious connection with agape, they have nothing to draw on, "not affection or principle enough to make them merciful or just, or to give them honour or compassion." Neither does anyone behave compassionately toward Maria's fiancé Mr. Rushworth, whom Maria neither likes nor respects but plans to marry simply because he's the richest man in the neighborhood. When Rushworth and Mary Crawford happen upon Thomas and Maria rehearsing "exactly at one of the times when they were trying *not* to embrace," Mary short-circuits the miserable fiancé's dawning insight by disingenuously noting of Maria's role "there is something so *maternal* in her manner, so completely *maternal* in her voice and countenance." When Sir Thomas's sudden arrival puts an end to the rehearsals, the intensified erotic tensions are left unresolved. Maria pulls back from the brink of breaking her engagement; once married, she is "glad that she had secured her fate beyond recall." Rather than repenting her erotic adventuring, she is determined only "to behave more cautiously to Mr. Rushworth in future."

The sad conclusion of Maria's story serves as Austen's reminder of the destructive power that is unleashed when eros degenerates into libido in a world where philia lacks the courage to name reality, and agape is absent. After Maria's wedding, Henry pursues Fanny but makes no progress. He and Maria both end up in London for the winter social season, where, away from their families' watchful eyes, their flirtation develops into a full-fledged sexual affair, which is quickly discovered. While the illicit lovers pay the price for their indulgence, Austen doesn't blame them exclusively for their disordered lives and loves. Instead, she traces the Bertram family problems to a broader failure of philia and of their failure to recognize and negotiate the tension between indulgence and repression. Reflecting on Maria's adultery and Julia's elopement with an unsuitable young man who can nonetheless be integrated into the family, Sir Thomas takes some responsibility for his adult daughters' behavior. Too late, he realizes that he had unwittingly taught the girls "to repress their spirits in his presence, as to make their real disposition unknown to him," and thereby increased the appeal of their superficial Aunt Norris, "sending them for all their indulgence to a person who had been able to attach them only by the blindness of her affection, and the excess of her praise." Maria and Julia's parents, following the practice of their time and class, had substituted abstract principles for the cultivation of agape. Their daughters "had been instructed theoretically in their religion, but never required to bring it into daily practice," and had never learned "the necessity of self-denial and humility."

Similarly, Austen portrays Henry Crawford not as an evil person but as a fairly ordinary one, "ruined by early independence and bad domestic example." Rich, left to his own devices, without guidance, he's seduced by vanity—a common flaw that can lead any of us into encounters we would do better to avoid. Austen's description of what could have been Henry's happier lot makes it clear that we need community if we have any hope of growing into truly loving persons: "Could he have been satisfied with the conquest of one amiable woman's affections . . . in working himself into the esteem and tenderness of Fanny Price, there would have been every probability of success and felicity for him." Instead, once he's in London, far from the friends at Mansfield Park who might have challenged him, Henry picks up his pursuit of the now-married Maria. He sacrifices his own chance at joy, not for any higher goal, but simply for the challenge of trying to "make Mrs. Rushworth Maria Bertram again in her treatment of himself."

Like Henry, Maria could have had the best this world can offer—all the loves lived in community—but she fares the worst of all the novel's characters. She seems condemned to a Hell worthy of Sartre. Her husband divorces her, and her father establishes a home for her abroad, where Mrs. Norris joins her and, as Austen observes, "it may be reasonably supposed that their tempers became their mutual punishment." Dante, remembering the last-moment conversion that gained Buonconte admission to Purgatory, would say that the fact that Maria is still alive offers some hope, but her ultimate fate is left to the reader's imagination.

The closing sections of *Mansfield Park* bring Fanny and Edmund together under the sign of the chain and the cross. The process is set in motion by their responses to the erotic chaos around them. The news of Henry and Maria's affair devastates Fanny, who thinks first of its impact on their family and friends: "Whom would it not injure? Whose views might it not affect? Whose peace would it not cut up for ever?" Austen makes it clear that for Fanny and Edmund, philia doesn't mean standing up for family no matter what. Fanny calls the affair "a sin of the first magnitude," and Edmund agrees; agape names the acts that rip apart bonds of love, and requires repentance as the first step to re-weaving them. But Mary calls the affair simply "folly," and wants to hush it up and bring Henry and Maria back into society as soon as Maria can be divorced and the two of them married. That suggestion ends her relationship with Edmund. He can't believe Mary is recommending "a compliance, a compromise, an acquiescence, in the continuation of the sin," and she accuses him of preaching to her. Lobbing a class insult that Austen's original readers would have instantly understood, she predicts that "when I hear of you next, it may be as a celebrated preacher in some great society of Methodists, or as a missionary into foreign parts."

As always in Austen's version of Purgatory, philia points the way. Finally facing the truth about the spiritual gulf that gapes between him and Mary Crawford, Edmund finds that "Fanny's friendship was all he had to cling to," and he talks out his pain and disillusionment to her all summer. Fanny feels sorry for him but, as Austen astutely remarks, "it was with a sorrow so founded on satisfaction" about the way to Edmund having been cleared "that there are few who might not have been glad to exchange their greatest gaiety for it." For Austen, deep friendship and agreement about fundamental values are the basis for a lifelong relationship, and eventually—"exactly at the time when it was quite natural that it should be so, and not a week earlier"—Edmund realizes that's what he shares with Fanny. Her "mind, disposition, opinions, and habits" are everything he could desire, not to mention Fanny's "soft light eyes." In Austen's world, that's hot.

Emma: Repression, Repentance, Forgiveness

If Austen had followed the pattern she started with *Pride and Prejudice* and *Sense and Sensibility*, she could have called *Emma, Repression and Repentance*. Attractive, intelligent, rich, and utterly lacking in self-awareness, the heroine of Austen's only novel named after a person rather than a place or idea is an amiably demonic presence who inflicts erotic chaos on everyone around her. To call Emma Woodhouse demonic may seem extreme, but it's an accurate description of the constellation of psychological and social forces that make her the most psychologically modern of Austen's heroines. Refusing to acknowledge eros as a force in her own life, Emma repeatedly imagines, and attempts to orchestrate, fantasy scenarios in which her friends take on the burden of her repressed erotic energy. In a slightly different world, or in the hands of a slightly different writer, Emma's machinations might well have spiraled into tragedy. It's not all that difficult to imagine Harriet Smith following Ophelia to her watery grave, one of the love triangles exploding into violence, or Dickensian versions of Jane Fairfax and Mr. Knightley living out their lives in embittered isolation.

Austen, of course, doesn't consign Emma to keeping Lear company on the blasted heath of regret: *Emma* is a dispatch, not from Hell, but from Purgatory. Like Dante, Austen shows how philia, grounded in compassion and a commitment to telling hard truths, has the power to free us from the erotic snares in which we trap ourselves. Although Emma's wealth puts her in a different situation from the young women in *Pride and Prejudice*, Austen's central point hasn't changed. The union between Emma and Mr. Knightley follows the pattern set by Elizabeth and Darcy. What *Emma* adds is an intimate, and absolutely contemporary, picture of erotic confusion and the psychology of purgatory. Most of us—it's tempting to say all of us if we're honest—have been in Emma's position: self-righteously convinced of our moral superiority, knowing that everyone else's view of the world is askew, while we see clearly. The specifics of our behaviors have changed somewhat over the centuries, but as Dante knew and Emma finally learned, in order to grow, we need to repent and forgive.

For Austen, the two terms are interwoven. Repentance is more than just feeling, or even saying, you're sorry; forgiveness more than waving away the past. They aren't things you do out of unthinking obedience, self-abnegation, or expediency. In *Amazing Grace: A Vocabulary of Faith*, Kathleen Norris offers an apt metaphor that illuminates Austen's approach: repentance means admitting that our spiritual and moral house is a mess and setting about making it "into a place where God might wish to dwell." Forgiveness is about relationship, the process of creating beauty in partnership with other flawed human beings. It's the starting point of an ongoing commitment to building the kinds of communities in which all the loves can thrive. We forgive in part because we hope we'll be forgiven, but more importantly, because it's what agape—the deepest, truest love—requires.

Emma certainly has much to repent. There's no need to belabor her multifarious mistakes, missteps, and misjudgments. A plot summary of the novel reads like a catalogue of her sins—again, not too strong a word for actions that threaten her community and compromise her integrity. Mistress of the snap judgment, Emma constantly projects her unconscious desires onto those around her and then proceeds to treat the fantasy as reality. Her groundless belief that the demure, decorous Jane Fairfax is the central figure in a love triangle involving her patron Mr. Dixon is one of the most egregious examples. Although Emma frequently feels mild regret over the failure of her schemes, her journey is filled with half-measures and false starts; twice, Austen specifies that Emma feels sorry, but "could not repent." But for all Emma's failings, we like her. Treating her with patience and ironic sympathy, Austen educates her readers about the process that makes repentance and forgiveness possible. *Emma* models the process it describes, guiding us to a deeper understanding of the need to empathize with our failed brothers and sisters, to pay attention to one another, and to support each other as we work through our shortcomings.

At the root of Emma's problems is her willful naiveté concerning the power of eros, especially as it affects her judgment. Repeatedly, she declares herself above desire. "I would rather not be tempted. I cannot really change for the better," she announces. "If I were to marry, I must expect to repent it." Expanding on her self-granted immunity, she tells her companion Harriet, "I have none of the usual inducements of women to marry. Were I to fall in love, indeed, it would be a different thing! but I never have been in love; it is not my way, or my nature; and I do not think I ever shall." The line between naiveté and repression is barely visible, as she projects her desires onto others, concocting a series of erotically charged plots straight out of Harlequin romances.

What results is a spectacular muddle that eventually teaches Emma she can't move other people around like chess pieces on a board of her design. Directing her considerable creative energy toward fantasy, Emma reduces her friends—Harriet, Jane, Frank Churchill, even Mr. Knightley—to actors in her erotic schemes. The pattern is set in Emma's treatment of Harriet, whose situation as the "natural daughter" of an unnamed father highlights the problem of unrestrained eros. For Emma, Harriet is as a social commodity, "whom she could summon at any time to a walk." She blithely assumes that Harriet's beauty will overwhelm the staid Mr. Elton, and lectures Mr. Knightley that Harriet is, "in fact, a beautiful girl, and must be thought so by ninety-nine people out of an hundred; and till it appears that men are much more philosophic on the subject of beauty than they are generally supposed; till they do fall in love with well-informed minds instead of handsome faces, a girl with such loveliness as Harriet, has a certainty of being admired and sought after." Beauty certainly does have value on the marriage market, but in this case as in others, Emma won't or can't see beneath the surface. The fault she projects onto "men" is really her own.

The collapse of the plot to marry Harriet to Mr. Elton teaches Emma roughly nothing. After a brief cooling-off period, she sets about concocting a new set of erotic intrigues centered on Harriet and Frank Churchill. When Frank "rescues" Harriet from gypsies she has come upon in the forest, Emma plugs her friends into a plot worthy of a gothic novel: "Such an adventure as this,—a fine young man and a lovely young woman thrown together in such a way, could hardly fail of suggesting certain ideas to the coldest heart and the steadiest brain ... How much more must an imaginist, like herself, be on fire with speculation and foresight!—especially with such a ground-work of anticipation as her mind had already made." Only the most befuddled of Austen's readers will be surprised when Emma's expectations again come to naught.

Once again, the key to Emma's blindness is her belief that she herself is immune to the power of eros, a theory she develops in detail during her flirtation with Frank Churchill. Even as she acknowledges that she is a little in love, she spins out a fantasy that leaves her in full control of the erotic game: "as she sat drawing or working, forming a thousand amusing schemes for the progress and close of their attachment, fancying interesting dialogues, and inventing elegant letters; the conclusion of every imaginary declaration on his side was that she *refused him*." Certain that Frank is more deeply attached then she is, Emma assures herself of her control: "I am quite enough in love. I should be sorry to be more." The whole thing will end as a minor episode in the life of a rich woman who doesn't *have* to marry and can't think why she would put herself to the trouble. "I shall do very well again after a little while—and then, it will be a good thing over," Emma reflects, "for they say everybody is in love once in their lives, and I shall have been let off easily."

She isn't, of course. In the final third of the book, Austen shifts attention from Emma's plotting—her "sins"—to her repentance. In that turn of events, Knightley plays the role of a secular Beatrice to Emma's Dante, combining an unswerving commitment to philia with a realistic awareness of eros. He repeatedly cautions Emma that her willful naiveté is a danger to herself and everyone around her. He warns her that Mr. Elton is in love with her, not Harriet, and that Frank is trifling with her to mask his involvement with Jane Fairfax. Accepting that philia means being honest even—especially—when that's difficult, he confronts Emma after she has humiliated her poor, talkative neighbor Miss Bates: "This is not pleasant to you, Emma, and it is very far from pleasant to me; but I must, I will,—I will tell you truths while I can, satisfied with providing myself your friend by very faithful counsel, and trusting that you will some time or other do me greater justice than you can now."

Emma's response to Knightley demonstrates the constructive role eros can play in the purgatorial consciousness. Motivated in part by the love she's just beginning to acknowledge, Emma feels deep shame over her behavior: "She was most forcibly struck. The truth of his representation there was no denying. She felt it at heart. How could she have been so brutal, so cruel, to Miss Bates!—How could she have exposed herself to such ill opinion in any one she valued! And how suffer him to leave her without saying one word of gratitude, of concurrence, of common kindness!" Emma would previously have retreated into self-justification, but now she experiences her first moment of real repentance. Understanding that she has to act on her awareness, Emma sets out to visit Miss Bates. Austen describes the walk in terms that make its purgatorial significance clear: "She would not be ashamed of the appearance of the penitence, so justly and truly hers."

That humble, sincere gesture marks the beginning of a journey that mixes joy and pain, as it did for Dante's pilgrims. For Emma, the joy is connected with the awakening of eros. When Knightley hears of Emma's visit to Miss Bates, Austen's language comes alive with the code words of desire. "He looked at her with a glow of regard. She was warmly gratified—and in another moment still more so, by a little movement of more than common friendliness on his part—he took her hand;—whether she had not herself made the first motion, she could not say—she might, perhaps have rather offered it—but he took her hand, pressed it, and certainly was on the point of carrying it to his lips—when, from some fancy or other, he suddenly let it go!"

Before the promise—the union of eros and philia—can be fulfilled, Emma must undergo a series of intensely painful events caused by the misfire of her plot to match Harriet Smith with Frank Churchill.

Discovering that Harriet has misunderstood Emma's fantasy and cast Knightley rather than Frank as the leading man, Emma is shocked into erotic self-awareness. "A few minutes were sufficient for making her acquainted with her own heart. A mind like her's, once opening to suspicion, made rapid progress. She touched—she admitted—she acknowledged the whole truth. Why was it so much worse that Harriet should be in love with Mr. Knightley, than with Frank Churchill? Why was the evil so dreadfully increased by Harriet's having some hope of a return? It darted through her, with the speed of an arrow, that Mr. Knightley must marry no one but herself!"

At that moment, Emma feels like she's in Hell. Lacking any real experience with eros or repentance, she's swept up in a torment of self-condemnation. For the first time, she understands her actions not as unfortunate mistakes, but as sins: actions that have compromised the fabric of her community. While not factually inaccurate, her assessment of her behavior is utterly lacking in the compassion the souls in Dante's Purgatory give one another. "With insufferable vanity had she believed herself in the secret of everybody's feelings; with unpardonable arrogance proposed to arrange everybody's destiny . . . she had done mischief. She had brought evil on Harriet, on herself, and she too much feared, on Mr. Knightley." Without a community to share their stories and provide perspective, she abandons hope. "The blunders, the blindness of her own head and heart!—she sat still, she walked about, she tried her own room, she tried the shrubbery—in every place, every posture, she perceived that she had acted most weakly; that she had been imposed on by others in a most mortifying degree; that she had been imposing on herself in a degree yet more mortifying; that she was wretched, and should probably find this day but the beginning of wretchedness." Othello would have understood.

Fortunately for Emma, the world she's living in has more in common with Shakespeare's comedies than with *Othello* or *Romeo and Juliet*. The sequence that culminates in Knightley's proposal begins with Emma in a vortex of erotic anxiety. Having acknowledged her love for

Knightley, Emma feels a profound remorse and begins the process of repentance. Focusing her thoughts on philia rather than eros, she thinks first of those her actions have harmed. As she passes through Purgatory, Emma's thoughts are couched in the language of the seven deadly sins, especially pride and envy. Thinking of her mistreatment of Jane Fairfax, Emma "bitterly regretted not having sought a closer acquaintance with her, and blushed for the envious feelings which had certainly been, in some measure, the cause." Sure that her failure to live in the spirit of philia has placed her beyond the reach of forgiveness, Emma—always the imaginist—spins out a bleak story in which she loses the friendship of Jane, Mr. and Mrs. Weston, Knightley, even Harriet and Robert. "All that were good would be withdrawn," she thinks. "What would remain of cheerful or of rational society within their reach?"

Even as Emma resigns herself to her lonely fate, she knows all is not lost. Part of her realizes that repentance has set her on a new spiritual path, so that "the only source whence any thing like consolation or composure could be drawn, was in the resolution of her own better conduct, and the hope that, however inferior in spirit and gaiety might be the following and every future winter of her life to the past, it would yet find her more rational, more acquainted with herself, and leave her less to regret when it was gone." Although Emma feels sorry for herself and imagines her past, present, and future as a closed circle, in fact she's in a spiral and has already begun her ascent. The pain she feels is the purgation Dante experienced: it's real and necessary, but it doesn't last forever and it's the gateway to spiritual growth.

The turning point comes for Emma when Knightley intrudes upon her "loneliness" and "melancholy" with news he assumes will pain her: Jane Fairfax and Frank Churchill are married. What follows is an intricate dance of eros, repentance and, finally, forgiveness. Already aware of the news and essentially unaffected by it, Emma surprises Knightley by thanking him for his friendship and acknowledging that she seems "to have been doomed to blindness." To her surprise, the gesture elicits a muted erotic response: "For a moment or two nothing was said, and she was unsuspicious of having excited any particular interest, till she found her arm drawn within his, and pressed against his heart." His gesture sparks a "flutter of pleasure," which she quickly checks. Making it clear that she has no interest in Frank, she offers to reciprocate the philia Knightley has given her by listening to what she imagines will be Knightley's confession of his love for Harriet. "If you have any wish to speak to me openly as a friend," she says, "as a friend, indeed, you may command me.—I will hear whatever you like. I will tell you exactly what I think."

Fearing that Emma's repeated emphasis on *friend* is a rejection— philia *not* eros rather than philia *plus* eros—Knightley vacillates before allowing eros to speak. "As a friend!" he begins, the rhythm of his words enacting an intense erotic drama. "Emma, that I fear is a word—No, I have no wish—Stay, yes, why should I hesitate?—I have gone too far already for concealment.—Emma, I accept your offer—Extraordinary as it may seem, I accept it, and refer myself to you as a friend;—Tell me, then, have I no chance of ever succeeding?"

The rest is comedy, human more than divine. Their torments transformed into mutual joy, Emma and Knightley arrive as close to the earthly paradise as anyone gets in Austen's world. Their joy is real, an image of the happiness that's possible when honesty and compassion bring eros and philia into alignment. The lovers travel through Purgatory together: "Within half an hour, [Knightley] had passed from a thoroughly distressed state of mind, to something so like perfect happiness, that it could bear no other name. *Her* change was equal.—This one half hour had given to each the same precious certainty of being beloved, had cleared from each the same degree of ignorance, jealousy, or distrust."

Austen doesn't confuse that half hour with eternity. Her description of the lovers' bliss is tinted with a sly and sympathetic irony. "Seldom, very seldom, does complete truth belong to any human disclosure: seldom can it happen that something is not a little disguised, or a little mistaken; but where, as in this case, though the conduct is mistaken, the feelings are not, it may not be very material.—Mr. Knightley could not impute to Emma a more relenting heart than she possessed, or a heart more disposed to accept of his." It won't be the last time that Emma and Knightley—or for that matter, Frank and Jane, Harriet and Robert, or the rest of us living out our lives in a world where blindness and deception so often reign—will be in need of a relenting heart. The ending, like those of *Pride and Prejudice* and *Mansfield Park*, as well as *A Midsummer Night's Dream* and *As You Like It*, is "happy," not "happily ever after": a moment of equilibrium and harmony in a process Austen knows will be longer and more complex. But just as Dante emerged from Purgatory "remade" and "ready to mount to the stars," Austen's characters come through their trials prepared to live in love and happiness together. In this life, that's the greatest blessing there is.

Al Green

CHAPTER FOUR

"'It's You I Want, but It's Him that I Need,' or, Imagining Paradise with The Reverend Al Green"

From the outside, Al Green's life looked like Heaven. It was 1974, and the slender singer with a voice as sultry as a slow kiss in summer shade seemed to be living love's dream. Simultaneously soothing and stimulating legions of fans with "Let's Stay Together," "Here I Am (Come and Take Me)," and "Tired of Being Alone," he had surpassed whatever idea of success he carried with him when his devout father threw him out of the house at age eighteen for listening to "the devil's music." Being alone was the least of his worries; staying together was for lyrics, not life. "Not only was I pleased to make acquaintance of every young woman who managed to sneak backstage, or through the hotel lobby, or into the back of the tour bus," Green later reflected in his autobiography, "but I considered it my due, a fitting offering to my natural-born charisma." "I wasn't," he admitted, "paying much attention to the laws of God and the wages of sin."

Then, early in the morning of October 18, in not much more than the blink of an eye, Green's Heaven turned to Hell. His reckoning arrived in the form of Mary Woodson, a lover who wanted more than he was willing to give. Midway through an evening recording session, Green had received a call from the Memphis sheriff telling him Woodson had been arrested for smoking marijuana at the posh Peabody Hotel. Cashing a few of the chips he'd accumulated doing charity work, Green negotiated Woodson's release and took her back to the studio. As he tried to calm her by singing his most recent hit, "Sha-La-La (Make Me Happy)," he was surprised by the arrival of a flight attendant paying a visit on a mid-South stopover. Attempting to defuse the tension, Green invited both women to his home, emphasizing that "the last thing on my mind... was some kind of kinky encounter."

"Safe inside my own four walls," Green showed the flight attendant to the guest quarters and returned to find Woodson stirring a large pot on the kitchen stove. Overlooking the fact that she'd left a husband and children behind in New Jersey, she suggested they get married. "Maybe," he answered, "we should talk about this in the morning." She kissed him and told him not to worry, things would be fine. Relieved to have made it through a difficult night, Green retired to his bathroom to prepare himself for sleep. As he bent down to finish brushing his teeth, the door opened behind him, and he glimpsed Mary Woodson's face in the mirror just before she dumped the boiling grits, a.k.a. Memphis napalm, on his back. Leaving him to writhe in agony, she shot herself to death with a pistol Green kept next to his bed.

It was a moment straight out of Dante's Inferno, an undeniable message that what might have looked like love was really libido: warped, destructive, divorced from philia and agape. While that terrible night wasn't the only turning point in Al Green's conversion from soul superstar to urban Pentecostal pastor, it was a key moment in the process that set him on a better and truer path.

The call to join him on that path, to bring the three loves into harmony, echoes through every stage of Green's career. Whatever he's singing, whether he's crooning, shouting, or whispering, the message is the same, and it comes from an eternal source beyond himself: "Stop. Listen. I'm with you, I love you, and I'll connect you with your true self and with other people." In the deepest of those connections, eros, philia, and agape intertwine, bringing us as close to Paradise as any living being can come. But to see the way ahead, Green's music tells us, we have to lift our eyes, step off the road we're on, reach out to others, and turn toward a new path together. In that hopeful, urgent message, there's no room to equivocate about sex and love. Eros is a powerful force for beauty, and so it will be present in Paradise, but if it's not intertwined with philia and agape, it's not true love. That's the lesson Dante learned on his pilgrimage, and it's one Al Green has preached in his music and learned in his life.

"I Was Turned Around": Al Green's Conversion

As he lay in the hospital recovering from third-degree burns, Green had plenty of time to think about the ways he had toyed with the objects of his erotic attention. The long-time girlfriend he'd pimped to white businessmen in the days before his success; the woman who'd charged him with assaulting her with a bottle; the adoring fans whose bodies he'd used without a thought for their minds or souls. And about a voice he'd heard in the California night, calling him to leave the false Paradise of libido and materialism and commit himself to a life that was deeper, truer, infinitely more fulfilling. He'd ignored the summons for months, and now, reflecting on where he'd been and imagining where he wanted to go, he was ready to answer the call.

It's tempting to see the grits incident as the defining moment in Al Green's conversion, but no matter how good a story that would make, it wouldn't be the whole truth. Conversion's more complicated than that, as anyone can testify who's made a radical break with a soul-destroying past—or a way of life that just wasn't working anymore. Conversion is a movement, not a moment, one that requires us to confront uncomfortable truths about how we've been living. As both recovering addicts and born-again Christians learn, it's an ongoing process in which a force outside ourselves empowers us to break the chains binding us to old, destructive ways.

Al Green calls that force the Holy Spirit. He first felt its pull as a child growing up in Arkansas, but resisted it for years. "Of course, there's lots of stories about how a man will turn from his wicked,

wicked ways, get right with God, and spend the rest of his days laboring to bring in the harvest," Green observed when he was well into middle age. "The Bible is full of them and I believe every one. But I'm not a fool. I know that being born again is the beginning of the journey, not the end." Like Green, all of us advance, slip back, feel torn between the competing impulses he felt as he stood at the crossroads in the 1970s. "I could continue to chase after the treasures dangled in front of my eyes. Or I could turn aside, walk away, and begin again. I did what most of us poor frail humans do. I tried to have it both ways."

More than a year before he met Mary Woodson, Green had been sleeping in his hotel room after a performance at Disneyland when he was awakened by the sound of shouting. Disoriented, he had the feeling he'd heard the voice before. It took him a few moments to realize the cries were his own. "I was praising God and lifting my voice to Heaven with the language of the angels," he remembered. "The Holy Spirit is a witness to what I'm saying—I'd never felt like it before. I went around knocking on people's doors, telling them, 'Hey! I've been saved.'" That morning, "everything was different." Green telephoned his parents to share the news, "and we rejoiced. We cried, and we rejoiced." In Green's words, "I was born again . . . I was converted, or changed about, or turned around, which is what converted means, to be turned about. And I felt so good, so perfect, so uplifted, so forgiven, so clean."

But even at the height of his inspiration, a second voice entered his awareness, "calm and clear, coming from inside me, but rattling the walls like a ten-point earthquake." The voice, Green wrote, came from Jesus. "'Are you ashamed of me?' was the question it asked and the words pierced me like a knife." Green's answer wasn't as clear as he would have liked. Powerful forces—fame, money, family needs—drew him away from the new path ahead. The morning of his born-again experience, Green decided his career was something he couldn't walk away from: "I was looking ahead to at least a solid year of concerts booked in advance. I had a multi-album recording contract to fulfill and a staff to support that now included members of my own family. Whatever else I might have felt like doing—such as basking in the warm glow of God's love for a few weeks while the world sorted itself out—was definitely going to have to wait." Like Dante at the moment Virgil declares him "free, upright, and whole," Green wanted to continue the journey to Paradise, but he wasn't yet clear on what it would actually take to walk that difficult path.

As it had been for Augustine, the young man and future bishop who prayed "Make me chaste, but not yet," libido was Green's primary impediment. In the months between Disneyland and the harrowing incident in Memphis, he equivocated, doing his best to keep eros— or a warped version of it—and agape locked up in different rooms. Losing himself in the endless cycle of concerts, publicity appearances, and recording sessions, he continued to accept the attentions of eager women, Mary Woodson among them. Even after her suicide, and his release from the hospital following an eight-month convalescence, he continued to grapple with "the age-old dilemma that puts a poor man between singing for God and singing for the devil." After a couple more years pulled in both directions, Green went on retreat: "I did me some fasting and praying. I rented a cabin next to a stream. No phone, no TV, no Coca-Cola. I didn't eat for forty days. 'Lord, what are you trying to do to me?'" That conscious emulation of Jesus' forty days in the wilderness in preparation for his ministry resulted in Green's decision to buy the modest church building that became his church, the Full Gospel Tabernacle. Even then, it would take a third event—a plunge off the edge of a stage at a 1979 concert in Cincinnati—to complete the conversion that had begun six years before. At the end of his second lengthy hospital stay, Green abandoned secular stardom to embrace his two vocations of pastor and gospel music singer. In our terms, he committed himself to living the three loves in balance: to imagining what the Paradise Dante saw would look like here on earth.

Turning Toward Paradise

There's a reason we're writing about *imagining* Paradise with Al Green. Like Dante, Green doesn't expect to fully experience Paradise—complete communion with the divine, other people, and all creation—until his earthly life has ended. That ecstatic union is a fervent, but future, hope. Yet that hope has immediate and urgent implications for how Green—and anyone who shares his vision—lives each day, here and now. It makes no sense to imagine a future of blissful contemplation of God—ultimate good, endless creativity, and deepest love—if we don't open our present lives to that unsettling force. Picturing ourselves in a heavenly choir of angels is an empty vision if we aren't willing to do the hard work of loving our neighbors in this world, even the show-offs and the ones who sing out of tune. A blissful reunion with lovers, family, and friends in the afterlife is a faint hope if we don't learn how to integrate eros with philia and agape in our daily relationships with them, and with those we'd rather forget—ex-spouses, ex-lovers, ex-spouses' ex-lovers, and all.

Al Green's life story attests that he's no angel. He's flesh and blood like all of us, with all the promise and peril that implies. He hasn't integrated eros into his life in the way he deeply desires. Married and divorced twice, the father of six children born over the course of twenty years, he would like to find a partner for the rest of his life. As Green told *Jet* magazine in 2008, "I would love to get married again. Because I am the Love and Happiness man, so I should be married." Quoting the song, he remarks, "Love will make you do right. I want to do right. I hope to get married to that special someone. Everybody needs it." Green's vision of the ideal marriage reflects the inseparability of friendship and passion, eros and philia: a spouse is someone "who's got your back, who is on your side, appreciates what you are doing and has a love for the same things. Two people who are going in the same direction, that's what I need." Aside from a few such comments, Green is famously reserved about his private life, devoting his considerable gifts and energies to articulating a hopeful vision through his preaching and music, and embodying it in his church community.

The Paradise Al Green's music calls us to imagine, and to live into, can be a reality in this life: full of flawed and faithful people, who rejoice in eros and do the hard, sacrificial work of keeping it connected to philia, who know it has to be grounded in agape, and who guide each other when—definitely not if—the way forward seems lost. Just as the one-time soul star grew into maturity through his multi-stage conversion, his work calls all of us to continue to grow in love, like the saints in Dante's Paradise who are filled with the divine presence and yet continue to deepen their communion. Few of us share Green's charisma or his gifts; many of us lack his secure faith; some reject the church because of its political history. But all of us need and can give love—and can start right now, wherever we are. Speaking from his faith tradition and his own experience, in song and sermon, Reverend Green asks each of us what we're waiting for, and he wants us to know it's not too late to let ourselves be turned around.

Walking with Jesus, Wandering in the World

A parable of the human quest to reconcile eros and agape, Al Green's struggle to heal his fragmented soul reflects a deep-seated pattern in the African American traditions that have shaped his life and music. Reflecting on the tension between the secular and the sacred, Saturday night and Sunday morning, Green wrote: "Black people in America have always been torn between walking with Jesus and wandering in the world, clear back to the times of slavery when we either cried out in captivity by singing the blues or held out for a better hope by singing spirituals." For Green, the music is centered in a vision of redemption that is simultaneously personal and political. "The church and the roadhouse have always been two stops on our long road to liberation, and we've been walking the line for hundreds of years. It's only natural that some of us lose our balance once in a while. That struggle is part of what makes us great as a people. . . and part of what makes our music so powerful." You can hear the tension between wandering and walking with Jesus in the soul songs that catapulted Green to stardom; in the gospel music he embraced after fully accepting his conversion; and in the twenty-first-century concerts where he infuses "Love and

Happiness," "Let's Stay Together," and "Tired of Being Alone" with a Spirit-filled energy.

Green's sense of the connection between the temple and the street was forged at a storefront church in Grand Rapids, Michigan, where his family moved when he was nine years old. The House of Prayer pastored by Mother Bates consisted of little more than a make-shift pulpit and a few rows of chairs, but what Green remembered was the agape-filled philia radiating from the gap-toothed woman with a crown of frizzy gray hair. "There was no derelict drunkard so lost he didn't deserve a good meal; no ratty and worn-out streetwalker too forlorn to reach with a loving touch; no chip on the shoulder of a tough kid that wouldn't melt at her words of love or the promise of her prayers," Green recalled. "It's no wonder that Mother Bates' storefront church was the hub around which the life of our neighborhood revolved. There was hardly another place along those dark and dingy streets where a searching soul might come for comfort and rest and a way back to the unconditional love of God."

Wrapped in the "freedom and serenity" of the community, and no doubt attracted by the echoes of eros in the tambourines and ecstatic movements that filled the church, Green gained a sense of his own voice for the first time. He'd begun singing in a group with his brothers, imitating the latest radio hits, but in the House of Prayer, he experienced something liberating and new. "I could really let go, without having to worry about hitting the right notes for the Greene Brothers harmonies or trying to sound just like Jackie [Wilson] or Sam [Cooke] or any other musical heroes I'd been drawn to on the radio. In those times, with two brothers behind me, banging out the rhythm on an old bass guitar and a snare drum, I was washed away in a flood of grace coming down from heaven, right through Mother Bates, and out across us all like a cleansing tide."

However powerful the force he found in gospel music, Al Green wasn't immune to the lures of the world. Like thousands of other young singers who'd been trained in the gospel church, he clashed with his father over his interest in "the devil's music" and set out in search of stardom and the rewards it could bring: money, cars, fine clothes, fine women. Like many of those others, he found himself drifting away from the church; soon he was looking at it from the outside. Struggling to get his career off the ground, he joined the Creations, a soul band that built its repertoire around "Jackie Wilson songs and James Brown moves." The band went nowhere, and, at the end of 1967, Green found himself with "No car. No phone. No fixed address," and a resumé that topped out at "sometime singer in a hometown soul band."

That was when he met Juanita, a beautiful prostitute who took him into her one-bedroom apartment and, in effect, recruited him as her pimp. Juanita, Green wrote, "will always occupy a place in my life directly opposite from, but equally important to, Mother Bates. They are like two magnetic poles, forces that kept me in balance between them, the one calling me to the purity of the faith, the other to the pleasures of the flesh. I make no judgment, nor do I cast any condemnation. As Mother Bates was born to her work, so was Juanita, and if circumstances had been a little different for either one of them, they might have found themselves in switched places." His family and the House of Prayer distant memories, Green found himself prowling infernal alleys and clubs where every imaginable pleasure was up for sale. "I could tell you the going price for a bag of weed just by smelling it, or how your cocaine had been cut with a taste on the tip of my pinkie . . . And if you couldn't afford the good stuff, I knew every cheap high under the sun, from rug lacquer to airplane glue . . . I could tell you the sexual preference of each regular customer, which prosperous white businessman liked to dress up in women's underwear and which one liked to be tied up while Juanita talked sass and dropped cigarette ashes on his head."

That life couldn't last, not without killing his soul, and it didn't. Aware that his relationship with Juanita was "held together as much by force of habit as by love or affection," and that both of them were wandering in a spiritual desert, Green left. His summary of their life together sounds cold or clear-eyed depending on your perspective: "She was a full-time whore and I was her part-time pimp and, between us, we had nothing to be proud of." Knowing he couldn't save Juanita, and afraid that if he stayed he "would never again see the light of day," Green took a new path. He split with the Soul Mates, the band he'd hooked up with after leaving the Creations, and dropped the "e" from the end of his family name, a first symbolic step in the decade-long journey to a new life. Shortly thereafter, he recorded "Back Up Train," which gave him a medium-sized regional hit on the R&B charts.

More importantly, the record drew the attention of Willie Mitchell, a long-time stalwart of the Memphis music scene, who would play the role of music industry Virgil to the singer's Dante. In late 1968, Mitchell's band was doing a brief tour in support of his hit "Soul Serenade." A producer in Midland, Texas put together a soul revue, and Green signed on for next to nothing. Wanting to hear a "familiar West Tennessee voice" and hoping to make an impression, Green approached Mitchell only to hear him dismiss "Back Up Train" as "tryin' to make somethin' out of nothing.'" With those words echoing in his head, Green climbed the stage to sing his hit, and haltingly took the musical step that would define his stardom. Green "started off soft, just barely making myself heard above the band, but then, instead of building up to some high, dramatic climax, I *kept* it soft and low, pronouncing each word carefully, drawing out the suspense, teasing out the meaning."

That's a precise description of the style that would make Al Green the voice of love. Understated, inviting, gentle, it burned with an intensity that spoke to something beyond the body's heat, something that couldn't be named openly in the musical world Green was desperate to break into. Looking back, Green credited the change with "Willie Mitchell's inspiration, pure and simple." He felt that he'd been brought to the Texas roadhouse "on this night of all nights for a very particular reason. I couldn't have told you what that reason was—the vision I'd been gifted with did not extend that far—but the certainty that Mr. Willie Mitchell and I were meant to meet brought with it a great peace and calm."

Nonetheless, like Dante at the beginning of the Inferno, Green's first response was to hesitate when the newly impressed Mitchell approached him. When Green asked how soon Mitchell could make him a star, the experienced producer answered honestly that it would take a year or a year and a half. "My heart sank," Green remembered. "*A year and a half!* I thought, *Why doesn't he just say it'll take an eternity.*" He was, like Dante, moving too fast to see the path in front of him. The voice of reason, Mitchell told Green that when he was ready, he'd be waiting. Back home in Michigan, unable to translate "Back Up Train" or his new voice into commercial success, contemplating the prospect of descent into an even deeper abyss, Green made a final break in his on-again, off-again relationship with Juanita. A few months later, he was in Memphis, knocking on Mitchell's door. Two years after that, right on the older man's schedule, Al Green was a star.

Between *Green Is Blues* (1969) and *Have a Good Time* (1976), Green and Mitchell collaborated on ten albums, six of which reached number one on the R&B charts while garnering "A" or "A+" ratings in Robert Christgau's *Village Voice* "Consumer Guide," the most influential source of reviews for the predominantly white counterculture audience. While Green's public image rested primarily on the singles that were fixtures on Top Forty radio, his albums tell the fuller story of his increasingly complex meditation on the tension between walking with Jesus and wandering in the world. Comparable to the volumes of poets like W.B. Yeats or Adrienne Rich, each album tries on a variety of voices while circling around a set of core concerns that evolve over time. In Green's case the connecting theme was the need to link eros with philia and agape.

Assembled as a showcase for the hit single, which reached number one on both the pop and R&B charts, *Let's Stay Together* (1972) establishes a point of departure for Green's quest. The album frames love almost entirely in terms of the relationship between two people: the gentle determination of the title song; the heartbreak of "So You're Leaving"; and the bluesy "It Ain't No Fun to Me," which ends the album with Green standing by the highway in the rain, counting the costs and wondering what went wrong. There's a strong sense of the need for healing energy in "How Can You Mend a Broken Heart," an awareness of eros's deeper roots in "What Is This Feeling," and even a distant echo of the revival standard "Old Time Religion" in "Old Time Lovin.'"

By the time he released *Al Green Explores Your Mind* (1975) and *Al Green Is Love* (1976), Green had experienced his Disneyland epiphany and was beginning to think more deeply about what it was he'd been seeking for so long. The first song on *Al Green Explores Your Mind*, "Sha-La-La (Make Me Happy)" makes it clear that Green hasn't forgotten about eros, but his vision of happiness has deepened. After blurring the line between sex and spirit with "Take Me to the River," he moves agape into the spotlight with "God Blessed Our Love," before investigating the tension between the blues impulse of "The City" and "One Night Stand" and the gospel impulse of "I'm Hooked On You" and "Stay With Me Forever."

His first fully realized statement on the union of the three loves, *Al Green Is Love* masks the spiritual message sufficiently to maintain Green's place in a pop music world notorious for resisting songs with openly religious lyrics. The opening track, "L-O-V-E (Love)" sounds the theme which Green expands in "The Love Sermon," "There Is Love," "Love Ritual," and "I Gotta Be More (Take Me Higher)," with its echoes of Jackie Wilson's gospel soul hit "Higher and Higher" and the Staple Singers' "I'll Take You There." Five years earlier, the goal had been to take a lover to the bedroom; now it was to live a life in which all the loves were united, in sunshine and in shadow, by daylight and by candlelight.

Just as Dante had to leave Virgil on the threshold of Paradise, Green's increasing focus on his religious vocation brought an end to his collaboration with Willie Mitchell. Aware that he was entering territory unfamiliar to his friend and mentor, Green took over production duties on *The Belle Album* (1977), a secular record in name only, whose surrender to agape would remain at the center of the two dozen gospel albums Green would release over the next two decades. From the plaintive title cut to the ethereal harmonies of the final track, "Dreaming," he keeps his eyes firmly on the prize of a "love that will last forever." A few years earlier, that might have sounded like a (probably successful) come-on line cut from the same cloth as "One Night Stand." On *Belle*, the soon-to-be-Reverend convinces you he's talking about the marriage of eros and agape, a truly lasting human love blessed by the divine.

The Belle Album signaled the beginning of the second major stage of Green's career, one in which he would address himself almost exclusively to the predominantly black world of gospel music. The criteria for success in gospel differ radically from those in popular music. Only truly exceptional gospel releases sell a quarter as many records as run-of-the-mill pop hits; and even the biggest African American gospel stars remain all but unknown in white America. While every Al Green fan can summon "Call Me" or "I'm Still in Love with You" effortlessly to mind, only a tiny percentage own copies of his Grammy-winning albums *The Lord Will Make a Way* (1980), *Higher Plane* (1981), *Precious Lord* (1982), or *I'll Rise Again* (1983). Few outside the core gospel audience can sing along with Grammy-winners "Going Away," "As Long as We're Together," or "Everything's Gonna Be Alright," let alone "You Brought The Sunshine" and "I Feel Like Going On," both of which could have been huge hits in a slightly different musical world.

Which is no doubt part of the reason Green reentered the secular market, at first cautiously, then whole-heartedly, at the start of the new millennium. Faced with the expense of running a church, he needed the money. Beyond that, one way to bear witness to the power that had led him away from the brink of Hell was to reach out to those still in danger, or at least in need of spiritual comfort. Green had sprinkled versions of spirit-tinged pop hits like "Put a Little Love in Your Heart," "You've Got a Friend," and "He Ain't Heavy, He's My Brother" on his gospel albums during the 1980s and 1990s, but it wasn't until 2003 that he reunited with Willie Mitchell on two albums, *I Can't Stop* and *Everything's OK*. *Lay It Down* followed in 2008, a looser, more relaxed compilation produced by hip-hop percussionist ?uestlove Thompson, on which Green collaborated with younger soul singers who had grown up with his music.

The best part of Green's return didn't take place in the recording studio. The real pay-off happened on stage, on occasions like the steamy summer night Craig saw him at the House of Blues in Chicago or the frigid evening in Little Rock that provided the opening scene for this book. Mesmerizing his long-time fans and those who hadn't been born when the hits (which a few might have been conceived to) were on the radio, Green now sings "Love and Happiness" and "Let's Stay Together" alongside his gospel hits and covers of classic songs by The Temptations and the Soul Stirrers. When questioned by *Rolling Stone*, he offered a good-humored defense of the hybrid performances: "God says the old songs are fine. 'I gave you the songs, Al. You can sing them if you want to.'" It's an affirmation of his belief that all beauty comes from God, even when we misunderstand or misuse it, as Green did back in the day. On his path from the Inferno to a place where he could glimpse Paradise, he had to withdraw from the old music for a while, to give agape the room it needed to bring the loves into balance. But when he found that balance, he could again enjoy the eros of the soul songs, knowing he wouldn't forget what he'd learned. The message of Green's new musical sermon was clear: the problem isn't that God doesn't want us to enjoy eros; it's that we all too frequently isolate it from the other loves and let it devolve into lust.

"Truth Is Light": Dante, Augustine and the Full Gospel Tabernacle

Al Green learned to live in better balance among the three loves, and helped teach those lessons, at the Full Gospel Tabernacle, a refuge a few blocks off Elvis Presley Boulevard in Memphis, Tennessee. Like Dante, he'd found himself, around the mid-point of his life's journey, "in a dark wood where the straight way was lost." And like Dante, Green followed a persistent call and an outstretched hand to a place where forgiven sinners live in community with each other, in the light—

and burning fire—of the Holy Spirit. Those who don't share the two artists' faith might call that disturbing, comforting force by other names: truth, commitment, or deep, generous love. However we name it, it's a force that urges us on to a place where the hope of a better life is real; where we can lean forward into that hope, and embody it in the way we treat each other. It's the energy that powers the profoundly personal, but inherently communal, journey that gives us glimpses of Heaven.

Both Dante and Al Green know that human beings can resist the call of the Spirit for a very long time, and they share a deep appreciation for the Christian belief that Jesus descended into Hell after his death. Like Shakespeare, Green is conscious of the risks and the temptations that pull us down: "In my own history, it seems I've made that descent many times, into a dark and smoky chaos only to be raised up again, with proclamations of resurrection and eternal life pouring from my lips. I don't know that I've ever seen heaven, except maybe in a vision or a dream. But I can tell you for sure that I've seen hell and lingered there among the damned." At the same time, Green shares Dante's awareness that even those misspent days can spur a wanderer on toward a better path where he or she can be transformed into a pilgrim who feels compassion for those still trapped in a life they would like to leave behind. Green is faithful, and clear-eyed, enough to know he hasn't reached Paradise yet. But his spiritual odyssey as musician and pastor nourishes the hope that all of us may glimpse what the pilgrim Dante saw fully: a community where we live the loves in balance, finding freedom and joy in communion with the divine and with each other.

It took Green years to find that community. When he was first born again, he didn't cancel his tour, but he did begin attending church every Sunday, "regardless of where I might find myself, or in what condition." He paid little attention to denomination or ethnicity, later remembering that "on occasion, I'd even end up with some Korean or Spanish congregation where, even if I didn't understand the words, at least the Holy Spirit was there to welcome me." As he wrestled with the call to devote his life to God, "those quiet and serene times I spent in churches were the highlight of my week."

The problem, as Dante could have told Al Green, was that he was following an essentially solitary path. He wasn't yet part of a faith community, and he was still resisting being wholly turned around. Eventually he realized that "God wasn't entirely satisfied with me paying Him a visit once a week. He wanted to invade my *whole* life and He wasn't waiting for an invitation." On tour, Green found himself spontaneously breaking into preaching and lengthy Bible quotations, feeling pushed by a force stronger than himself, his heart racing, his voice not under his control. He didn't want to let down the people depending on him, or lose the wealth and fame he'd worked so hard for, "But at the same time, I couldn't turn my back on the God who had come in visitation and asked with a voice that cut at my heart, 'Are you ashamed of Me?'" After years of resistance and struggle, it was time for Green to witness publicly to the changes that had happened in his soul, and to live the life they called him to.

And so he got off the road and took a new path, as full-time pastor of the Full Gospel Tabernacle. His prayer of thanksgiving about that pivotal moment might shock some, but it's likely to resonate deeply with far more: "The Lord lifted me. I'd run so fast and for so long, and I was so tired. Thanks be to God. Thanks be my lucky ass!!" That prayer is no pious platitude about his soul being saved, and going to Heaven when he dies—although Green believes deeply in both. It's an expression of deep gratitude for having been prodded to give up what he thought he wanted, in order to receive everything his heart truly desired. Among those who will affirm that prayer are converts to various faiths, veterans of twelve-step programs, refugees from Wall Street, and parents who have left jobs outside the home.

Green's vision of perfection integrates the physical and the spiritual, the temporal and the eternal, and it's lived out in a modest community of working people who each have their own conversion story, whether it's less, or even more, dramatic than their pastor's. Green testifies to the Full Gospel Tabernacle's role in his own ongoing conversion: "God delivered me from the Egypt of my own vanity and pride and delivered me to the humblest of circumstances, a place where I could discover, for the first time in my life, the spiritual rewards of sacrifice and service. Like Moses sitting on the slopes of that rocky old mountain, carefully watching over Jethro's flock, so too I was brought to a lowly station to minister to the needs of the poor of spirit, those called blessed in the Beatitudes." The stage is no longer Green's primary platform: when he's in the pulpit, he's preaching rather than performing, leading worship among people who have come together in vulnerability and in strength, who are pledged to offer, and ask for, support when it's needed. The underlying rhythms of Green's life have been transformed: "Where before my days were spent in bringing my name before crowds of strangers, either chasing after fame or trying to hold on to it, now the seasons rolled by in rituals of baptism and marriage and funerals and the hundred other simple milestones that mark the lives of ordinary folks." The pastor's life he describes isn't a profitable venture. Green is no preacher of the prosperity gospel that proclaims God's blessings can be measured in dollars, and whose prophets often command high salaries. He supports his family and his ministry by touring, but for years his church and singing lives have been integrated: the same band and singers work with Green in church and on the road. Their work and worship, and their secular and spiritual lives, are interconnected in a way that's not fathomable in a profit-driven world, but that's absolutely essential to Paradise.

The Tabernacle's Pentecostal faith is centered in a deep personal relationship with God: Father, Son, and Holy Spirit. While the three persons of the Trinity are inseparable, believers think of the Spirit as the one who allows them to experience God's presence and to live their lives in response to the divine call. The Pentecostal movement traces its modern origins to the early twentieth-century Azusa Street revival in Los Angeles, but its roots extend back to the day of Pentecost after Jesus' ascension to Paradise. On that day, the Book of Acts says, the apostles received the gift of the Holy Spirit: "Divided tongues, as of fire, appeared among them, and a tongue rested on each of them. All of them were filled with the Holy Spirit and began to speak in other languages, as the Spirit gave them ability." Pentecostals like Al Green expect to receive the same gifts the first Christians did: speaking in tongues and interpreting them, prophecy, healing, preaching, teaching. These gifts can come suddenly to an individual, as Green experienced at Disneyland, but usually they're given in communal worship, which lasts for hours filled with music, preaching, and souls testifying to the power of God. To outsiders, Pentecostal worship can seem chaotic and fragmented, but church members have learned a powerful lesson: when the Spirit seizes you, you have to give yourself up to it. And sooner is better than later. That relationship will bear fruit, not only in worship, but in lives transformed by subtle and precious gifts like love, joy, peace, patience, generosity, and self-control. Together, the church forms a community of praise, hope, and freedom, where believers trust the Spirit's power to bring about physical, emotional, and sexual healing.

No one knows better than Al Green that the community never trusts perfectly in the power of love. The church can, and often has, fostered fear of eros in the name of striving for perfect agape. But Green has sought a more unified way, rooted in his deep belief in the goodness of all divine gifts including sexual love, and his appreciation for the vital and complex role black churches have played in his people's history. Years into his pastorate, he reflected on the church as the "hub" around which his family's life revolved: "It's a tradition that dates back to slavery times, when church was the only place my people could gather together and be themselves, hidden from the eyes of the overseer. That sanctuary only grew in importance for blacks as time went on, and it was in church that our hopes were elevated, our community consolidated, and our spirits regenerated."

The Full Gospel Tabernacle extends that agape-suffused philia to the strangers who crowd it on Sundays hoping for a glimpse of its famous minister in what has again become his natural habitat. When writer Scott Spencer visited the church in 2000, a member asked guests to stand, whereupon "A scattered crew of Japanese, French, German and out-of-town Americans" were greeted with the words, "We welcome you. We love you. And may God bless you." Spencer notes that the church's iconography is as diverse as the visitors and its home congregation: "There are two murals displayed. One shows wrecks on the highway—trucks and cars overturned, a jet crashing into the top of a building—and the souls of the departed zooming up to the sky, where a white Jesus awaits them. The other shows an African-looking Jesus walking on water."

The simple act of depicting both a white and a black Jesus on the walls of the Full Gospel Tabernacle demonstrates the church's commitment to creating a community grounded in the most inclusive love there is, as a counter-cultural witness in a world where so many relationships are based on the power of some to control others. Green believes his church attracts people other churches haven't reached, who may arrive on its doorstep because of the pastor's reputation and charisma, but who stay, or go on to find a church in their home community, because of the hope they find there. The church web site expresses that hope, and the pastor's hard-won conviction that conversion is a process. On the site, Green invites visitors to "Ask [Jesus Christ] into your life today. By confessing your sins, you will be given the miraculous gift of salvation. Your burden will ease and the clouds will begin to part." There's no promise that whatever burden you're carrying will instantly disappear, or that you'll live every day in sunshine; simply that you'll have company and sustenance on your journey and that, whenever it ends, it will end joyfully. Green calls the life of faith the church offers "Power for living," and visitors to the web site will see it expressed immediately in three ways: invitations to worship, to call the church's prayer line, and to contribute to its food bank—or receive assistance from it. Green sums up his approach to ministry in a simple statement: "At least you can be there, to be what the people need at the time when they need it."

Reaching out to those in spiritual and material need is central to the Full Gospel Tabernacle, whose pastor sees himself first of all as an evangelist. For Green, the church is called to be a community "multiplying blessings," following in the footsteps of their ancestors in faith and reaching out to new generations. As an ordained leader, Green has consciously assumed the mantle of an elder, striving to integrate the loves in all aspects of his life and to lead his people in doing the same. He's not offering society's solutions to love's dilemmas, the strategies he used for so long with tragic results: repression, denial, commodification, or indulgence. When young people arrive at his church, Green notes with a smile, "Maybe there's been some fornicating," but the church works with them to redirect their passions. That acceptance, and the promise to accompany others as they walk the often steep path that leads to higher ground, is rooted in Green's conviction that the three loves can't be separated. He exhorts others and himself: "[We] need to corroborate 'I love you Lord' with 'I care about you, my fellow man.' The commandment is 'Love thy neighbor!', so I can sing 'Let's Stay Together' with all that it means. What do you want me to sing, 'let's stay apart'? No, if we love each other, then we can be reconciled with God and be perfect."

Al Green knows the stakes in this quest are high, and he also knows it's not up to him to choose the path anyone else will follow, or to judge the road they take. The call to conversion, healing, and new life is ultimately mysterious. Sounding like the Tunisian bishop Augustine—like Green a member of the African diaspora that has played such key roles in shaping both the church and non-Christian communities—Green reflects, "Who can say why one man is born again and another stays dead in his sins? Who knows why God picks one and passes over the other? None of us can say what the plan of God may be for our lives, the number of our days, or the purpose to which they will be put. But I do know this: the choices we make follow after us, lifting us up or dragging us down. God may choose you or me or anybody He pleases. But we have to choose back, every minute of every day. Every time we say yes to Him, we climb a little closer to heaven. And every time we say no, we drop a little farther toward hell. In His mercy, he leaves it up to us."

Those who aren't drawn to Christianity may wonder: is everyone who isn't "born again" as Al Green was, doomed to stay "dead in his [or her] sins"? Green doesn't presume to judge the ultimate fate of any soul, but as an evangelist his mission is clear: to preach the Gospel in music, words, and deeds, scattering seeds that may bear fruit in transformed lives. We know, and no doubt Green does too, that some of those lives are transformed outside the church. You don't have to be Christian, or a person of faith, to understand the need for community, but the kind of community Green's pointing toward isn't just any group of people who choose to associate with each other. By definition, it's *not* a club or an interest group. It's highly challenging and deeply rewarding, because it's shaped by selflessness, informed by the desire to live a more whole life for the sake of everyone's children, not just our own. And it has to include people who don't necessarily like each other or get along well, but who recognize that they need, and can learn from, each other. For those who don't share the Christian identification of agape with God, the challenge is to identify what kind of community that could be.

Calls and Responses: An Al Green Mix

Grounded in the African American tradition of call and response, Al Green's music—sacred, secular, country, or old school soul—explores questions of what it *really* means to intertwine the three loves in our lives. The exploration Green invites his listeners to participate in isn't linear. It's a life-long engagement with the visions of the cultural, literary and spiritual ancestors who shepherd us through our hardest days and darkest nights. Accepting their guidance, arguing when we disagree, we can develop creative ways to shape communities that will illuminate love's liberating potential and imagine ways of incarnating that love in the world.

The process of call and response provides a way to connect our individual stories without denying their specificity. Reflecting on her experience, one person sends out a call—a song, story, painting, dance, anything that allows for honest expression of thought and feeling. Typically, the call invokes previous stories and images that embody the community's understanding of similar situations. References to *Romeo and Juliet*, the Song of Songs, or *Sex and the City*, for example, activate different clusters of erotic associations. Individual members of the audience respond out of their own experience: they can affirm the call, reject it, or say "yes, and," redirecting attention to things the original call overlooked. A strong response can become a call of its own, opening paths to new insights and awareness.

At their best, lovers do that for one another. The most intense moments of erotic connection, as Al Green's music affirms, take place when two people respond to one another's calls while remaining connected to circles of community and spirit. As their rhythms ebb and flow, their individual voices and bodies merge, creating something new that takes them deeper into a previously unimagined shared self. Eros, as the poet Audre Lorde writes, can release our creative energies, tapping "the power which comes from sharing deeply any pursuit with another person. The sharing of joy, whether physical, emotional, psychic, or intellectual, forms a bridge between the sharers which can be the basis for understanding much of what is not shared between them, and lessens the threat of their difference." During erotic communion, each person is not lost, but enhanced as she or he becomes part of something new and greater than the individual.

That's the energy at the core of Al Green's music: the rhythm, the vision, the call. You can hear the conversation between body and spirit unfolding in individual songs and in albums like *Al Green Is Love*, *The Belle Album*, and *Higher Plane*. But the best way to appreciate the fullness of what he has to say—to understand why Al Green and the tradition he represents belongs in the same conversations as Dante, Shakespeare, and Jane Austen—is to let the voices of his soul and gospel songs weave themselves around each other and to lose, and maybe find, yourself in the music.

Track 1: Love and Happiness

The keynote sermon of Al Green's life-long musical worship service, "Love and Happiness" boils the *Divine Comedy*'s vision down to 5 minutes and 3 seconds. Or, to translate Dante into the home vocabulary of African American music, it marks the place where gospel meets the blues. As Ralph Ellison put it in his essay on black novelist Richard Wright, the blues isn't a specific musical form, but an *impulse*, a strategy for dealing with pain, suffering, and despair. "The blues," Ellison wrote, "is an impulse to keep the painful details and episodes of a brutal experience alive in one's aching consciousness, to finger its jagged grain, and to transcend it, not by the consolation of philosophy but by squeezing from it a near-tragic, near-comic lyricism." Like the *Inferno*, the blues takes a hard clear look at human weakness. Brutal experiences may feel as if they simply happen *to* us, like visitations of malevolent forces. There *are* evil forces in the world: no one who reads history, or the daily news, can seriously doubt that. But more often than not, each of us does his or her part to spread the bad news. As bluesman Robert Johnson put it, "me and the devil was walking side by side."

Al Green is intimately familiar with the blues, and that's where "Love and Happiness" begins: at the moment when we mistake libido for love. Libido's pull can be overwhelming, and at 3 a.m. we may or may not bother to ask the questions we know we should. The rhythm in your heart and hands, the taste in your mouth and the smell in your nostrils, can pull you all the way over the edge into an abyss from which you may not escape. Sin, as Green knows, is real.

But he also knows it's not the whole, or only, story. The flip side of the blues, and the deepest source of the appeal of "Love and Happiness," is gospel. These two musical and poetic impulses have a lot in common. Just as the blues impulse begins with a brutal experience, gospel originates in the struggles of a man or woman who's been given a cross to bear. While the blues response to trouble is to sing out your pain, in gospel it's to bear witness, to testify to hope. The difference between the blues and gospel impulses lies in where they leave you. As

African American novelist Albert Murray wrote, "No wonder Hamlet came to debate with himself whether to be or not to be . . . Hamlet's [question] was whether things are worth all the trouble and struggle. Which is also what the question is when you wake up with the blues there again, not only all around your bed but also inside your head as well, as if trying to make you wish that you were dead or had never been born." Shifting the balance away from Shakespearean tragedy, the gospel impulse offers not just the ability to go on and face another blues-battered day, but also the hope of redemption, the vision of a better world, one in which personal salvation and social transformation aren't abstract ideas but embodied realities. As gospel singer Mahalia Jackson said, "Gospel songs are the songs of hope. When you sing them you are delivered of your burden . . . I tell people that the person who sings only the blues is like someone in a deep pit yelling for help, and I'm simply not in that position."

No question, Green understood that when gospel meets the blues, the devil has a lot of arguments ready to hand. That was a big source of Green's frustration in the years after his initial conversion, when he was still billed as a secular performer but would sing gospel and preach spontaneously from the stage. He wasn't dismissing eros, but trying to put it into perspective for his listeners. "You're supposed to have a companion—It's not good that a man should be alone. Go, be fruitful and multiply, children, all that, great," he told an interviewer. "But see, when you start talking to people about that in a club, after they've had about three or four joints, after a few martinis, a little Scotch on the rocks: Man, give me the chick, this is my neighbor's old lady right here, and we're just out for the party, see? Now you're going to tell me about the Law—we'll get to that on Sunday, OK?" Green's frustration, radiating a blues humor, is tempered by the fact that he made those same arguments himself for years; he's speaking from inside knowledge, not judging others from a safe distance.

But as "Love and Happiness" testifies, even when Green was face to face with the blues, he heard the gospel call and held out the possibility that at the end of our struggle, we can "walk away with victory." Riding the energy of the right-out-of-church organ and the erotic—not just sexual—responses of the backup singers, "Love and Happiness" pulls back from the abyss and points toward the path that Dante followed in the Comedy, and which, walking side by side with Al Green, we'll chart for the rest of this mix.

Tracks 2 and 3: Take Me to the River/None but the Righteous

No two songs better embody the call and response between eros and agape, or between the gospel and blues impulses, than "Take Me to the River" and "None but the Righteous." "Take Me to the River" is sultry, sweaty, straight-from-the-bedroom Memphis funk, but its lyrics could (just about) come from a Baptist hymn. When Green asks you to follow him down to the healing waters, it's not just your soul he has in mind. But it's not just your body, either: he knows the two can't be separated. Cut from the fade of "Take Me to the River" to the opening chord of "None but the Righteous" and you'll be hard pressed to know when, or if, you've crossed the line between secular and sacred. Both songs promise Heaven. The difference is that where the soul man is inviting you inside an erotic bubble to luxuriate in the liquid touch of skin on skin, the gospel singer knows that Heaven isn't a moment between the sheets. It's living your life in a community that shares the faith that love can change the world. The righteousness Green sings about isn't *self*-righteousness, calling down the wrath of God on those you believe are outside his embrace. It's knowing that even though you—and everyone else—are a sinner, God loves you—and everyone else—anyway, and has called you to a better life than what you had before, one in which, as Green sings joyously, we can "walk together, talk together, sing together, shout together." Together like the inhabitants of Jane Austen's country houses, who may not have shouted much, but who slowly became more skilled at loving each other in the spirit of philia and agape, allowing eros to assume its rightful, harmonious, place.

Track 4: L-O-V-E (Love)

Like Ray Charles, Green knew that you could draft a hymn into the service of seduction simply by substituting a woman's name for the Lord's. On his hit single "L-O-V-E," it's hard to tell whether eros or agape is singing lead. Propelled by the jubilant opening horn riff, Green announces that he started out writing a song to his lover but decided instead to dedicate it to the source of energy that reaches out from, and draws us toward, Paradise. While Green caresses each phrase, the background singers simply repeat *love love love*. It's not a lament like the echoing *eros* in the final scenes of *Antony and Cleopatra*, but a meditative affirmation that love is "what the world is made of," and a call to open your heart to the change that was coming in Al Green's music and in his life.

Track 5: Amazing Grace

It came as no surprise when Al Green included "Amazing Grace" on his 1981 album, *Higher Plane*. An eighteenth-century hymn written by John Newman, the captain of a slave ship (who, contrary to reassuring legend, didn't give up his trade immediately after his vessel survived a terrible storm), the song has resonated with millions, not only Christians, who knew their personal strength was nowhere near enough to bring them back from the edge, or sometimes the middle, of Hell. It's been sung by fugitive slaves; soldiers in trenches, jungles, and deserts; civil rights workers; and women in South African townships. Not to mention Mahalia Jackson, Johnny Cash, Judy Collins, Sam Cooke, Elvis Presley, Allen Ginsberg, the Royal Scots Dragoon Guards, Willie Nelson, Joan Baez, and Aretha Franklin, whose 1973 *Amazing Grace* remains the best-selling gospel album of all time.

When Green added his voice to the chorus, he wasn't trying to compete with Aretha, or anyone else. Disarmingly simple and lacking the vocal embellishments that defined both his gospel and soul records, his version is above all a heartfelt praise song to the lived reality of grace: the love we can't earn, buy, or barter for, only accept gratefully and generously offer to others. When Green sings the song's central lines, "I once was lost, but now am found, was blind, but now I see," he's testifying to grace's transformative power to change our view of reality. By the time he sang "Amazing Grace," Green, like Dante at the gates of Paradise, was learning to see the three loves, and his own life, in a new and different light.

Track 6: Surprise Attack/Highway to Heaven

"Surprise Attack," the first movement of a powerful gospel medley that was recorded more than a decade before being released in 1989, begins in darkness. Night's falling, the singer's soul is sleeping. In Dantean terms, he's lost in a dark wood. Against a slow beat, unsteady as a hesitant heart, Green begins to open his eyes. Drawing on the wellspring of the Pentecostal tradition, he channels the beautiful images of the second chapter of Acts: the wind, the flame, the unintelligible words that somehow make themselves understood. His voice tinged with soft wonder, he testifies to the brush of the mighty wind on his soul, the sound of a voice like many waters. A minute into the song, the rhythms have coalesced into joyous clarity, the sound of awakening souls moving forward, not in unison, but united.

As "Surprise Attack" segues into "Highway to Heaven," the bass settles into a propulsive syncopation and Green joins hands with his fellow pilgrims. A song that began in isolation transforms into a celebration of philia. Like the souls disembarking at the beginning of the Purgatorio and those in "None But the Righteous," Green's travelers are walking, talking, and singing together—a series of verbs that's repeated over and over in the Reverend's music—not just as lovers, but as members of a community of pilgrim souls seeking a higher, firmer, ground.

Track 7: Love Ritual

Some of those souls are with us in body: family, friends, lovers; members of our churches; teachers and students we meet sometimes in classrooms but more frequently, if we're paying attention, out in the larger world. Their embodied presence is precious. But, as Green testifies in "Love Ritual," the circles of philia aren't limited to the present time or the material world. Mixing the multi/omni/polycultural rhythms James Brown was spreading through the soundscape of the 1970s with the voices Green had heard in the Pentecostal church, "Love Ritual" reaches out to the elders, ancestors, and fellow seekers in every corner of the African diaspora. You can hear echoes of Nigerian griots Olatunji and King Sunny Ade, of salsa and samba, of Cuban percussion wizard Machito, of Aretha Franklin and her spiritual sisters La India, La Lupe, and Celia Cruz. Of Jacob dreaming while his head rests on a pillow of rock. Of the body and blood of Jesus flowing into the sacred wine and bread of communion.

There's no real point in trying to distinguish one voice, or current, from another. At the height of the musical intensity, Green cries out a series of indecipherable syllables and phrases, evoking the apostles at the moment they were touched by the Holy Spirit's tongues of flame. The many-layered texture of calls and responses is an affirmation that the Spirit isn't reserved for those who speak Aramaic or Greek or English. Eros and philia manifest themselves differently in different times and places but agape always works through them, calling us together rather than pulling us apart.

Track 8: People Get Ready

In the African American tradition that nurtured Al Green, walking and singing together had strong political implications. The story of the African American freedom movement extends back to Moses leading the Hebrews out of Egyptian bondage, fugitive slaves escaping from slavery to freedom, hundreds of thousands marching on Washington, black children joining hands and walking up the steps into newly, angrily desegregated schools. At every step, agape and philia gave freedom's warriors the strength to go on.

Redemption, the central image of "People Get Ready" and dozens of other songs that powered the African American freedom movement during the time Al Green was growing up, isn't simply personal. You can't use it as a cover for distancing yourself from the reality of oppression, willfully ignoring the burdens of the world. In our time when apologists for exploitation and oppression condone economic violence, educational institutions treat children as disposable objects, and too many Christians celebrate war in the name of the Prince of Peace, attempting to shrink Jesus into a pawn in a bumper sticker war, it's not hard to see why many people committed to social justice turn in disgust from what they see as a monolithic and irredeemable church. Christians like Green see their call differently. In the words of the gospel standard, they're determined to live the life they sing about in their songs, embodying Jesus' commitment to live side by side with the poor, the outcast, and the downcast, knowing they'll find Him among them.

Joining his voice with Mavis Staples on a quietly joyful version of the anthem Curtis Mayfield wrote and sang for The Impressions at the height of the civil rights movement, Green embraces the liberating tradition that flows from spirituals like "Go Down, Moses" and "No More Auction Block for Me" to the sermons of Reverend C.L. Franklin and the speeches of Martin Luther King, Jr. Along with Sam Cooke, Aretha Franklin, and Stevie Wonder, Staples and Mayfield created music that inspired the movement's leaders and gave strength to the ordinary people whose commitment turned abstract ideals into lived philia.

No song expressed their vision more clearly than "People Get Ready." The call is open to anyone willing to live in the light of the Spirit: "you don't need no ticket, just get on board." But that light's not soft; you can't hide in or from it: "There ain't no room for the hopeless sinner who would hurt all mankind just to save his own." The guitar solo that follows that verse in Green's version makes the last minute of the song—in which the two singers repeat the phrase "thank the Lord" over and over—all the more powerful. It's not a call to a warped charity, helping the "needy," which always involves a hierarchy that distances us from the objects of our usually self-serving benevolence. It's a reminder that we're all connected and need to behave accordingly, working together to create a world in which the voices of the "poor" are heard and heeded.

Track 9: Free at Last

Sometimes it feels like the path to a transformed life will never reach its destination, like the whole world's a wilderness. Sung in a somber voice that turns the hopeful peroration of Martin Luther King, Jr's "I Have a Dream Speech" into a meditation on the length of the journey, "Free at Last" borders on the blues. Half valediction for a love gone wrong, half homage to the fallen leader, the song carries the weight of King's murder, which was both a tragedy and a sin. By 1973, when Green released the song on the *Livin' for You* album, it was clear that the March on Washington hadn't led black people to the promised land. But just as Green knows the end of a relationship doesn't destroy the possibility of love, he shares King's belief that death isn't the end of life. Deep inside the sorrow, Green embraces the joy of the words that grace King's tombstone: "Free at last, free at last, Thank God Almighty, I'm free at last."

Tracks 10 and 11: I'm So Tired of Being Alone/ Everything's Gonna Be Alright

These two songs embody the call and response that shapes the arc of Al Green's musical life. The soul-deep desire for love, imagined as eros; agape holding out a beckoning, reassuring hand. It's the difference between longing for a Paradise that may not exist, and knowing it's real and expecting to find it. A syllable separates "love and happiness" from the "peace, love, and happiness"—as Green rephrases it in "Everything's Gonna Be Alright"—that comes to those who open themselves to the promise at the center of Green's faith: "He's coming back, like he said he would." With that future hope informing our current life, we can live in the light of Paradise now, knowing that even when we're by ourselves, we're never really alone.

Track 12 and 13: How Can You Mend a Broken Heart?/ You've Got a Friend

While Al Green's musical roots reach deep down into the soil of African American gospel and soul, he didn't hesitate to send out branches into country, rock, and pop, covering songs by The Doors ("Light My Fire"), The Box Tops ("The Letter"), Kris Kristofferson ("For the Good Times"), the Beatles ("Get Back," "Something"), Willie Nelson ("Funny How Time Slips Away"), the Hollies ("He Ain't Heavy"), and Hank Williams ("I'm so Lonesome I Could Die"), among others. On "How Can You Mend a Broken Heart," he transforms a wistful pop hit by the pre-disco Bee Gees into a bluesy sermon on the theme of getting through another long lonely night. Thinking back on a younger self devoted to personal pleasure, Green reflects on a life lived solely in the present tense: "I could never see tomorrow." Building on the churchy organ and soft snare drum that open the song, the long, trilling violin lines and the background vocals enfold Green's voice in a web of loss. Each voice speaks to an individual, indelible sorrow, but the fact that they're singing together is a reminder of philia, of the knowledge that burdens can be shared. From the halfway point on, Green all but abandons the song structure, turning the pop tune into an improvisational prayer. By the end, he's pleading *I just want to I just want to I just want to live again.*

The path back to life and love, as Green's remake of Carole King's "You've Got a Friend" tells us, is more likely to begin with philia than with eros. Stepping outside his defining roles—as lover/seducer or pastor/evangelist—Green offers the hand of gentle, accepting friendship he was himself seeking in "How Can You Mend a Broken Heart." It's no coincidence that "You've Got a Friend" has special meaning for the women who provide the bedrock of Green's audience and his church. One of the biggest hits from King's album *Tapestry*, which had been America's best-selling album for fifteen weeks during 1971, the song was equally familiar to Green's African American listeners from Aretha Franklin's *Amazing Grace* album. Blending the song with the gospel standard "Precious Lord Take My Hand," Aretha gave King her whole-hearted amen, then reminded her listeners that the source of all love is agape, altering King's final line—"All you have to do is call and I'll be there"—to "close your eyes and meditate on Him, soon He will be there." What matters for both Green and Aretha is the spirit connecting the singers with their communities. Like the souls in Dante's Purgatory, joined in the music of philia and agape, Aretha and Green reassure the (extra)ordinary women they sing to and for that they'll never be alone.

Track 14: Lay It Down

The hard-won peace that flows through Green's gospel albums stayed with him when he returned to the world of secular music at the turn of the millennium. You can hear it in the familiar grooves of the albums he made when he reunited with Willie Mitchell, which sound exactly like what they are: a reunion of old friends. Passion is involved, but the tone is familiar, comfortable, affirmation rather than discovery.

"Lay It Down," the title track of Green's 2008 collaboration with ?uestlove Thompson of the hip-hop group The Roots, makes it clear that comfort hadn't made Green complacent. In earlier years, Green and Mitchell had been perfectionists in the studio; most of the places where Green's voice soars and dips with seeming immediacy on "Let's Stay Together" and "I'm Still in Love with You" were put together phrase by phrase over dozens of takes. Overcoming his hesitation to interfere with Green's process, Thompson convinced his idol to work in a much more improvisational style. "Al Green could give most freestyle rappers a run for their money," the young producer observed. "The energy and excitement that you hear in his voice, him ad-libbing to himself, talking to us, laughing, that's just genuine excitement of what he never knew was still around, which was the *feeling* of the music." The results were spectacular. Singing in the relaxed, assured tones of an elder secure in his voice and vision, Green merged his voice effortlessly with neo-soul singers Anthony Hamilton, John Legend, and Corrine Bailey Rae, musical disciples carrying the vision of the three loves into the world of downloads, iPods, Pandora, and whatever comes next.

The high point of an album filled with Green's most memorable soul performances in three decades, "Lay It Down" radiates a profound, hard-earned wisdom. Riding Thompson's subdued drumming and engaging in a good-humored call and response with Anthony Hamilton—whose CDs *Comin' From Where I'm From* and *The Point of It All* are as close to *Let's Stay Together* and *Al Green Is Love* as the new century has to offer—Green sounds like a man who's found a place to rest and wants others to join him there.

Tracks 15 and 16: Sailing on the Sea of Your Love/ God Blessed Our Love

If Al Green had signed on to write the music for an opera based on the *Divine Comedy*, these two songs would be the soundtrack to the *Paradiso*. Like the ocean of light that dazzles the pilgrim Dante in Paradise, the sea Green sails in his duet with Shirley Caesar (one of the dozen or so greatest voices in the history of gospel) embodies both eros and agape-infused philia. Caesar, like Beatrice, draws her companion onward, offering reassurance and keeping his attention directed toward the higher prize. The song's erotic undertones are clear; a listener who didn't understand English would have no difficulty recognizing it as a love song, an expression of delight in the dance of male and female energies. That interpretation wouldn't be wrong, just incomplete. Like the final book of the *Comedy*, "Sailing on the Sea of Your Love" refocuses erotic energy on Jesus, the lover calling the soul home to God.

Where "Sailing" embraces the harmony of the loves, "God Blessed Our Love" captures the tension that keeps Dante's *Paradiso* from slipping into stasis. Like Dante singing the praises of his beloved, Green's song blurs the line between eros and agape. He's saying the right things; he means it when he assures his beloved that they have a love they can be proud of, that what they have is holy, not libido or lust. But for all that, both Green's voice and the music linger on lines like "I love holding you, I love kissing you" in ways that make you suspect he might be willing to settle for life inside the erotic bubble. When he sings "I can see Heaven in your eyes," you pause for a moment to ask yourself whether, like the religious rhapsodies of *La Vita Nuova*, those pretty words might be just a line.

At which point, in our hypothetical musical, Beatrice would chide her suitor, reprise "Sailing On the Sea of Your Love," and remind him that the proof of his love will be in the life he lives.

Track 17: Let's Stay Together

One of our goals in putting together this mix was to create a sonic tapestry that lets you come back to the standards and hear them in new ways. Try it now. The chances are good that anyone who's made it this far into our journey can bring "Let's Stay Together" to mind without much prodding, but it's worth calling it up on your iPod or slipping it into the CD changer. Give it three listens, each time with a different love in mind. *Eros.* Think about the irony of Al Green's women fans, swept up in the sensual moment, tearing at his clothes; of Green welcoming their overtures while singing the praise of a lasting union. The sound of Heaven wafting above a path leading, as Green learned, to the edge of Hell. *Philia.* "Let's Stay Together" may focus on two people—for Green a man and a woman—caught up in the throes of eros, but the yearning at its core speaks as deeply to those who aren't in the middle of a love affair. That may be why, while the song was being recorded, Willie Mitchell invited about 50 men from the neighborhood, whom he called "winos," into the studio and passed around a few bottles. When it comes to the desire for a lasting love, we're all—even those who may not appear to qualify as the "righteous"—in it together. *Agape.* The erotic frenzy and the communal longing will keep "Let's Stay Together" in the Top Twenty seduction songs for as long as anyone bothers to make lists, but what makes it immortal art, rather than pop fluff, is its connection to something higher and deeper. "Lovin' you *forever*": in the harmonies that wrap around Green's voice, the horns and strings that put air under the lyric's wings, the line promises and provides, a glimpse of Paradise; a love for all seasons, capable of weathering the storms of life. Absolutely erotic and absolutely divine.

Track 18: Belle

Part praise-song, part erotic valediction, "Belle," the title song from Green's last secular album of the 1970s, is the strangest of love songs: a poignant, perfect meditation on the journey from a lover's arms to a place of deeper peace. When Green called it "the most important song of my career," he was thinking of more than the delicate aching beauty that earns it a place alongside "Let's Stay Together," "Let's Get It On," and "I Never Loved a Man" in the pantheon of great soul ballads. Feeling the full power of the gospel blues, the burden of pain and the hope of redemption, Green turns from eros to agape with a bittersweet joy: "It's you I want but it's Him that I need." For a man who had experienced sensual pleasure as fully as Green, that need wasn't abstract. "The woman I'd been singing to might have been imaginary, but to me, she was every beautiful fan who ever wanted to get next to me," he reflected in his autobiography. "The sadness you can hear in that song is real, too. I loved those women, loved their softness and sweetness and the way they gave themselves away for the chance to be lost and found in love." But, he went on, "those days—and those ways—were past me now. God called me to a higher place, turned me away from earthly to Heavenly love, and while it hurt to say it, I had to leave the sensual for the spiritual."

Leaving, as we've been suggesting throughout *Love and Happiness*, may not be quite the right word. Maybe "journeying" or "transitioning," re-imagining the sensual as *part* of the spiritual, not its center but inseparable from it, one of the most beautiful rings of light shimmering through Paradise. The culmination of Al Green's musical mix, "Belle" calls us to a place where we can see and experience that beauty more fully. Where we can look back on the paths we've traveled and imagine new ways ahead. Where we can stand in the light of the Spirit with our guides beside us: contemplating the reality of sin and suffering and flickering redemption with Shakespeare; listening to Jane Austen as she turns her incisive and ultimately hopeful humor on the vicissitudes of life among our fellow seekers. Where we can accompany Al Green and Dante as they emerge from their journeys to stand in the light of what

"Belle," echoing a biblical image that has echoed down the ages and been attached to Jesus Christ, calls the "bright morning star."

As the final notes subside, leaving our responses to determine the meaning of the song—as they do with Shakespeare's plays and Austen's novels—we stand once more beside Dante in the final stanza of his Comedy. Bedazzled, amazed, and inspired, he turns to the hard work of living a life that will one day lead him back to Paradise, and to Beatrice. He can't fully describe what he's seen: "Here force failed my high fantasy," he writes in awestruck wonder, "but my desire and will were moved already—like a wheel revolving uniformly—by the Love that moves the sun and the other stars." Like the stars, love often seems impossibly far away, evading our touch, disappearing from time to time behind clouds that we fear will never part. But with Dante and Al Green, soul brothers across the centuries, we can trust that like the bright morning star, love will light our path and lead us to freedom as, together, we walk the pilgrim way.

Sources

The most important sources for *Love and Happiness* are, of course, the poetry, drama, fiction and music of our title figures. While we have read and value numerous translations of Dante's *Comedy*, we settled on Allen Mandelbaum's three-volume version, originally published by the University of California Press in the early 1980s and reprinted by Bantam in 2004. In addition, we referred frequently to the notes of John D. Sinclair's prose version, published by the Oxford University Press in 1939 and still the best single-volume English language gloss of Dante's numerous allusions. Citations from *La Vita Nuova* are taken from Mark Musa's translation (Oxford University Press 1999). For *Othello, Romeo and Juliet, Measure for Measure, A Midsummer's Night Dream,* and *Antony and Cleopatra,* we used the Folger Shakespeare Library texts edited by Barbara A. Mowat and Paul Werstine, but referred frequently to the volumes in the Oxford World Classics series, which include excellent overviews of the plays' performance history. Quotations from the Sonnets are from *Shakespeare's Sonnets,* edited by Katherine Duncan-Jones (Arden Shakespeare 1997). Quotations from *Pride and Prejudice, Mansfield Park,* and *Emma* were taken from the Penguin Classics editions. Our discussion of Al Green refers to songs from many different albums, all of which can be found on iTunes. Listeners coming to his music for the first time can get a sense of the shape of his career by listening to *Al Green Is Love, Let's Stay Together, The Belle Album* and *Higher Plane.*

Next to the primary texts, our most important sources have been the writers whose meditations on eros and spirituality set our conversations in motion: C.S. Lewis, *The Four Loves* (1943, reprinted by Harcourt 1960), and Octavio Paz, *The Double Flame: Love and Eroticism* (Harcourt 1993). As we began to investigate the theological understanding of eros, we turned to Augustine's *Confessions* as translated by Maria Boulding (New City Press 2002); Paul Tillich's *Systematic Theology* (University of Chicago 1951), which contains a brilliant discussion of demons; Alisdair MacIntrye's *After Virtue: A Study in Moral Theology* (University of Notre Dame 1984); and Kathleen Norris's *Amazing Grace: A Vocabulary of Faith* (Riverhead 1999). Throughout the project, we have been inspired by Ariel Bloch and Chana Bloch's translation of the *Song of Songs* with an insightful introduction by Stephen Mitchell (Modern Library 2006). Our understanding of the *Song of Songs* was shaped in part by the four volumes of Bernard de Clairveaux's *On the Song of Songs*, translated by Robert Walton. A sampling of Bernard's sermons can be found in *Selected Works*, edited by G.R. Evans (Classics of Western Spirituality 1987).

The biographical and critical literature on Dante, Shakespeare and Austen is enormous. Readers who want a path in are referred to the volumes on each in *The Cambridge Companion* series, each of which includes extensive bibliographical information. The Austen volume is edited by Edward Copeland and Juliet McMaster, the Dante volume by Rachel Jacoff, and the Shakespeare volume by Margreta de Grazia and Stanley Wells. The biographical sources that had the most direct impact on our discussions were Harriet Rubin's *Dante in Love: The World's Greatest Poem and How It Made History* (Simon & Schuster 2005); Stephen Greenblatt's *Will in the World: How Shakespeare Became Shakespeare* (W.W. Norton 2005); Rene Weis's flawed but provocative *Shakespeare Unbound: Decoding a Hidden Life* (Henry Holt 2007); Irene Collins's *Jane Austen: The Parson's Daughter* (Bloomsbury 2007); and Jon Spence's *Becoming Jane Austen* (Bloomsbury 2003), which is much more trustworthy than the movie based loosely on Spence's work.

Biographical information on Al Green was drawn primarily from Green's autobiography *Take Me to the River*, written with the assistance of David Seay (Harper 2000); the excellent DVD, *The Gospel According to Al Green*; and a variety of journalistic sources, most notably "Al Green: Rhythm and Blues Legend of 30 Years" (*Jet* 21 July 2008); and Scott Spencer's excellent "Al Green's Gotta Serve Somebody" (*Rolling Stone* 28 September 2000). Readers interested in the musical and cultural traditions that inform Green's music should begin with Anthony Heilbut's *The Gospel Sound: Good News and Bad Times* (Simon & Schuster 1971); the reviews of Green's albums in Robert Christgau's *Rock Albums of the 70s: A Critical Guide* (Da Capo 1981); Craig Werner's *Higher Ground: Stevie Wonder, Aretha Franklin, Curtis Mayfield, and the Rise and Fall of American Soul* (Crown 2004); and Albert Murray's *Stomping the Blues* (Da Capo 1976).

Our discussions of the historical understanding and contemporary importance of Dante, Shakespeare and Austen have been enriched by *The Cambridge Companion to Shakespeare and Popular Culture*, edited by Robert Shaugnessy; Eric Griffiths and Matthew Reynolds' *Dante in English* (Penguin 2005); the fascinating website, *Dante Today: Citings & Sightings of Dante's Work in Contemporary Culture*; Steve Chandler and Terrence Hill's *Two Guys Read Jane Austen* (Robert Reed 2008); *A Truth Universally Acknowledged: 33 Great Writers on Why We Read Jane Austen*, edited by Susannah Carson (Random House 2009); and Emily Auerbach's informative and amusing *Searching for Jane Austen* (University of Wisconsin 2006).

We have incorporated direct references to several critical books and articles: Diana Jean Chemo's "Bringing Dante Into the Realm of Contemporary English" (*New York Times* 31 January 1995), which includes Robert Pinsky's comments on Dante; Terry Eagleton's *William Shakespeare* (Wiley-Blackwell 1986); and Gail Kern Paster's "*Romeo and Juliet*: A Modern Perspective," published in the Folger Library edition of the play. Published more than a half-century ago, the two volumes of Harold Clarke Goddard's *The Meaning of Shakespeare* (University of Chicago 1951 and 1960) remain, to our mind, the gold standard for short introductions to each of the plays.

Index

Acts, Book of, 121-22, 131
addiction, 107
Ade, King Sunny, 132
adultery, 9, 42, 91
Aeneas, 14
After Virtue (Alisdair McIntyre), 77
agape, ix, x-xiv, 3, 5, 39, 54, 72, 73, 77, 126; defined, viii; Dante and, 4; in *Divine Comedy*, 12, 16, 19, 22-31; Augustine and, 10; Shakespeare and, 38; in *Othello* 42, 45, 46; in *Measure for Measure*, 47-50, 52, 53; in *Romeo and Juliet*, 58-60, 62-64; in *Antony and Cleopatra*, 64, 65; Jane Austen and, 75; in *Pride and Prejudice*, 85, 87; in *Mansfield Park*, 87-89, 91-93; in *Emma*, 95; and grace, 95; Al Green and, 106, 107, 109, 110, 111, 112, 122; in Al Green's music, 115-18, 129, 130, 132-34, 136-39
Allen, Woody, 40, 54
Ali, Muhammad, 79
All Night Long, 42

Amazing Grace (Aretha Franklin), 130, 135
Amazing Grace: A Vocabulary of Faith (Norris), 95
Amos (prophet), x, 126
Anglican church (see Church of England)
Antony and Cleopatra (See Shakespeare, William, Works)
Aphrodite, 68
Aquinas, Saint Thomas, 27
Ares, 68
Aristotle, 8
Augustine, Saint, 9, 30, 109, 118, 124
Austen, James, 77, 79
Austen, Jane, xii, xiii, 71-102, 126, 129, 139; images of, 71, 78-80; economic awareness, 72, 74, 77, 82, 83; adaptations and sequels, 72-3; and Purgatory, 74-78; biography, 75; and Church of England, 75-6; compared to Dante, 77; male responses to, 78; correspondence, 79, 81;

romance with Tom LeFroy, 80; view of marriage, 80-81; on childbearing, 81; view of clergy, 88

Works

Emma, 72, 94-102; demonic energy in, 94; repentance in, 95, 98, 100; psychological themes, 94-95; Emma's erotic scheming, 95-97, 99; theme of honesty, 97; Emma's self-awareness, 99; resolution of, 100; happy ending, 102

Mansfield Park, 72, 87-93, 102; religious themes in, 87-89; image of the cross, 87; harmony of the three loves, 87-88; role of clergy in, 88; marriage market in, 89; theatricals in, 90-91; failure of philia, 91; repression in, 91; resolution of, 93

Pride and Prejudice, 71, 72, 73, 74, 78, 82-87, 94, 102; film versions, 73; sexual energy in, 83; Lydia's elopement, 84; marriage theme, 85; economic themes, 86-87

Sense and Sensibility, 72, 78, 94

Characters

Bennet, Elizabeth, 81, 83, 84, 94; Bennet, Jane, 81, 83, 85-87; Bennet, Kitty, 73; Bennet, Lydia, 84, 87; Bennet, Mary, 73, 84; Bennet, Mr., 73, 83; Bennet, Mrs., 83; Bennet sisters, 72; Bertram, Edmund (*Mansfield Park*), 87-90; Bertram, Julia (*Mansfield Park*), 90, 92; Bertram, Maria (*Mansfield Park*), 90-93; Bertram, Sir Thomas (*Mansfield Park*), 89-91; Churchill, Frank (*Emma*), 96-99, 101-2; Collins, William (*Pride and Prejudice*), 82, 83, 85; Crawford, Henry (*Mansfield Park*), 87-93; Crawford, Mary (*Mansfield Park*), 88-91, 93; Crawford, Thomas (*Mansfield Park*), 88, 90-91; Darcy, Fitzwilliam, 72, 73, 82, 83, 85-87, 94; Fairfax, Jane (*Emma*), 94-97, 101-2; Knightley, Geo (*Emma*), 94, 96-102; Lucas, Charlotte (*Pride and Prejudice*), 85; Norris, Mrs. (*Mansfield Park*), 88; Price, Fanny, 87-93; Price, William, 87-88; Smith, Harriet (*Emma*), 94, 96-102; Woodhouse, Emma, 72, 94-102

Azusa Street Revival, 121

Baez, Joan, 130
Baldwin, James, xi, 127
Beatitudes, 121
Beatles, The, 135
Becoming Jane, 80, 81
Bee Gees, The, 135
Berlioz, Hector, 58
Bernard of Clairvaux, Saint (See Dante, characters)
Bible (see also individual books), x, 37, 51, 108, 120, 126

blues, 111, 116, 116, 127, 128, 129, 134, 135, 139
blues impulse, 116
Book of Common Prayer, The, 75, 89
Bosch, Hieronymous, 5, 13
Box Tops, The, 137
Bride and Prejudice, 73
Bridget Jones' Diary, 73
"Bring It On Home to Me" (Sam Cooke), vii
Brown, James, 113, 132
Byron, George Gordon, Lord, 73

Caesar, Shirley, 137
call and response, 125-26, 128-29, 132, 134, 137
Cambridge History of English Literature, The, 78
capitalism, 38
Cash, Johnny 130
Catholicism, 76
Catch My Soul, 42
Chandler, Steve, 78
Chaplin, Charlie, 54
Charles, Ray, 130
Charon, 17
Christgau, Robert, 115
Church of England, 39, 72, 75, 76
Churchill, Winston, 41
civil rights movement, 130, 132, 133, 134
Cleopatra, 14, 59; representations of, 66; Shakespearean character, 64-68
Clueless, 73
Collins, Irene, 75

Collins, Judy, 130
Coming From Where I'm From (Anthony Hamilton), 137
commodification, xii, 20, 38, 43, 47, 51, 61, 63, 64, 72, 75, 79, 86, 96, 124
communion, 75, 132
Companion to the Altar, A, 75, 76
compassion, 17, 19, 39, 46, 99, 101,
Comte-Sponville, Andre, xi
Confessions, The (Augustine), 10, 30
conversion, xii, 10, 106-9, 123, 124, 126
Cooke, Sam, vii, 112, 130, 133
country music, 125, 135
Cruz, Celia, 132

Dali, Salvador, 5, 13
Dally, John, 1
damnation, 6, 29,
Dante, ix, x, xii-xiv, 1-26, 36, 37, 45, 51, 60, 63, 66, 72, 74, 76, 77, 79, 89, 92, 94, 97, 98, 99, 100, 102, 106, 107, 109, 111, 114, 115, 116, 118, 119, 120, 125, 126, 127, 129, 131, 136, 137, 139-40; exile of, 4; modern response to, 5; attitude toward sin, 9; and Beatrice, 10-11; sins of, 18; experience of social chaos, 21; involvement in politics, 24; compared to Jane Austen, 77
Works
Divine Comedy, xii, xii, 1-31, 72, 127, 129, 137; opening scene of, 3, 11-12, 118, 131; erotic fantasy

in, 3; plot of, 4; Dante's guides, 4; modern responses to, 5; Italian references in, 7-8; Dante's relation to persona, 12; demons in, 13-14; final scene, 142

   Inferno, xiii, 5-6,9, 11-17, 18, 22, 36, 45, 47, 63, 77, 106, 115, 118 127; artistic portrayals of, 5; Canto I, 12; second circle of, 14, 66; lowest circles, 16-17

   Paradiso, xiii, 7, 25-31; Dante's reunion with Beatrice, 23-25; geography of, 25-26; music in, 27; Dante's parting from Beatrice, 27; St. Bernard in, 27-31; sphere of the Sun, 27; Empyrean, 29-30; Image of God, 30; Trinity in, 31

   Purgatorio, xiii, 6, 17-22, 134; seventh terrace of, 16; Dante's entrance into, 17-18; as church, 18; departure of Virgil, 22; music in, 17, 22, 23

   Vita Nuova, La, 10, 11, 15, 16, 23, 29, 60, 89, 138

Characters

   Beatrice, xiii, 3, 4, 10-14, 18, 21-29, 31, 37, 77, 90, 97, 137, 138, 140; Bernard of Clairvaux, Saint, xiii, 4, 27-31; Buonconte de Monfeltro, 19, 91; Daniel, Arnaut, 20-21; Eve, 29; Galleyhault, 15; Gianciatto, 17; Guinevere, 15; Guinizelli, Guido, 20-21; Jason 17; Judas, 17; Lancelot, 15; Lucifer, 17; Lucy, Saint, 12; Mary, Virgin, 12, 19, 29; Medea, 17; Paola and Francesca, 15-17, 21; Rachel, 12; Virgil xiii, 4,12, 13, 14, 16, 20, 21, 22, 27, 45, 77, 109, 114, 116; on types of love, 20

Dark Lady of the Sonnets, 41
democracy, 26
demons and demonic energy, xii, 13-16, 35, 56, 94
desert fathers and mothers, xi
Dench, Dame Judi, 40, 64
Devil (see also Satan), 9, 109, 127
Dickens, Charles, 94
Dickinson, Emily, 21
Dido, 14, 59
divorce, 86, 93
Donne, John, ix, 21, 40, 62
Doors, The, 135
Double Flame: Love and Eroticism, The (Paz), ix
Drabble, Margaret, 80

Eagleton, Terry, 37
East of Eden, 58
Elizabeth, Queen, 39, 40
Ellison, Ralph, 129
Emma (See Austen, Jane, Works)
Episcopal church (see Church of England)
eros, ix, x, xi, 5, 9, 36, 39, 54, 73, 75, 77, 126; defined, viii; Christian attitudes toward, xiv; Dante and, 3, 4; in the *Divine Comedy*, 12, 14, 15, 16, 17, 18, 20, 22, 23, 24, 25, 27, 28, 29, 31; Augustine

and, 10; Shakespeare and, 35, 37; as commodity, 38; in *Othello*, 42, 43, 46; in *Measure for Measure*, 47, 49, 50, 53; in *A Midsummer Night's Dream*, 54, 57; in *Romeo and Juliet*, 58-62, 64; violence and, 54-56; in *Antony and Cleopatra*, 64-68; Jane Austen and, 72, 74, 79, 80, 81; in *Pride and Prejudice*, 82-86; in *Mansfield Park*, 88-91, 93; in *Emma*, 94-101; Al Green and, 106, 107, 109-12, 122; in Al Green's music, 115, 117, 118, 128, 129, 130, 132, 134, 135, 137, 138-39; Audre Lorde on, 126

Essex, Earl of, 39

fate, 26
Faust, 2
Fiennes, Joseph, 40
Fitton, Mary, 41
"For the Good Times" (Kris Kristofferson), 135
forgiveness, 24, 46, 94, 95, 100,
Four Loves, The (Lewis), ix
Fowler, Karen Joy, 71
Franklin, Aretha, 130, 133, 135
Franklin, Rev. C.L., 133
free will, 26
Full Gospel Tabernacle, vii, 109, 118-24
"Funny How Time Slips Away" (Willie Nelson), 135

Gable, Clark, 40
Garden of Earthly Delights, The (Bosch), 13
Garson, Greer, 73
"Get Back" (Beatles), 135
Ginsberg, Allen, 130
"Go Down, Moses," 133
God, viii, ix, xiii, 4, 9, 14, 17, 18, 19, 24, 26, 27, 28, 29, 30, 31, 45, 49, 50, 54, 63, 105, 108, 109, 110, 112, 116, 118, 120, 121, 122, 123, 124, 125, 126, 129, 137, 139-40
Goethe, Johann, 2,
gospel music, x, 109, 111, 116, 117, 125, 127, 128, 129, 130, 133, 135, 136, 139
grace, 133
Green, Al, vii, x, xi, xii, xiii, 105-140; relation with father, 105; grits incident, 105-6, 107, 109; conversion, 106-9, 122, 128; and Full Gospel Tabernacle, 109, 118-24; biography, 110, 112-14; on sacred and secular in African American culture, 111; musical career, 113, 114-18; criminal activities, 113-14; vocation as pastor, 121, 124; on role of black church, 122

Albums
Al Green Explores Your Mind, 116; *Al Green is Love*, 116, 126, 137; *Belle Album, The*, 116, 117, 126; *Everything's OK*, 117; *Green Is Blue*, 115

Have a Good Time, 115; *Higher Plane*, 117, 126, 130; *I Can't Stop*, 117; *I'll Rise Again*, 117; *Lay It Down*, 117; *Let's Stay Together*, 115, 137; *Livin' for You*, 134; *Precious Lord*, 117

Songs
"Amazing Grace," 130-31; "As Long as We're Together," 117; "Back Up Train," 114, 115; "Belle," 117, 139-40; "Call Me," 117; "City, The," 116; "Dreaming," 117; "Everything's Gonna Be Alright," vii, 117, 134; "Free At Last," 134; "God Blessed Our Love," 116, 137-38; "Going Away," 117; "He Ain't Heavy (He's My Brother)," 117; "Here I Am (Come and Take Me), 105; "How Can You Mend a Broken Heart," 116, 135-36; "I Feel Like Going On," 117; "I Gotta Be More (Take Me Higher)," 116; "I'm Hooked on You," 116; "I'm So Tired of Being Alone," vii, 105, 112, 134; "I'm Still in Love with You," 117, 136; "It Ain't No Fun to Me," 115; "Lay It Down," 136-37; "Let's Stay Together," vii, 105, 111, 112, 118, 124, 136, 138, 139; "Lord Will Make a Way, The," 117; "L-O-V-E," vii, 116, 130; "Love Ritual," 116, 131-32; "Love Sermon, The," 116; "Love and Happiness," vii, 110, 111, 118, 127-29; "None But the Righteous," 129, 131; "Old Time Lovin'," 116; "One Night Stand, "116, 117; "People Get Ready, "132-34; "Put a Little Love in Your Heart," 117; "Sailing on the Sea of Your Love," 137-38; "Sha-La-La (Make Me Happy)," 105, 116; "So You're Leaving," 115; "Stay With Me Forever," 116; "Surprise Attack/Highway to Heaven," 131; "Take Me to the River," 116, 129; "There Is Love," 116; "What Is This Feeling," 116; "You Brought the Sunshine," 117; "You've Got a Friend," 117, 135-36

Gregory the Great, Pope, 8

Hall, Peter, 64
Hamilton, Anthony, 136-37
Hathaway, Anne, 41
Havens, Richie, 42
Hawking, Stephen, 41
Hawkins, Peter, 23
"He Ain't Heavy (He's My Brother)" (Hollies), 135
healing, 12, 18, 76, 124
Heaven (see also Paradise), xii, 2, 7, 13, 23, 25, 26, 51, 62, 63, 64, 105, 108, 112, 119, 120, 129, 139
Hell (see also Inferno), x, xii, 2, 4, 5, 6, 7, 9, 11, 13, 14, 16, 17, 18, 19, 23, 24, 31, 38, 42, 43, 45, 46, 47, 54, 63, 64, 67, 68, 72, 81, 92, 99, 105, 117, 119, 125, 130, 139

High School Musical, 58
Hill, Terrence, 78
hip hop, 138
Hollies, The, 137
Holy Spirit, xi, 107, 108, 119, 121, 122, 132
homosexuality, 8, 20
Hughes, Will, 41
hypocrisy, 75, 88

"I Have a Dream" speech, 134
"I Never Loved a Man" (Aretha Franklin), 139
idolatry, 21
"I'll Take You There" (Staple Singers), 116
"I'm Gonna Live the Life I Sing About in My Song," 133
"I'm So Lonesome I Could Cry" (Hank Williams), 135
Impressions, The, 133
incest, 14, 50, 89
indulgence, x, xi, xiii, 65, 84, 86, 91, 124

Jackson, Mahalia, 128, 130
Jacob, 132
Jane Austen Book Club, The, 71, 73
jazz, 57
jealousy, 35, 42, 43, 44, 47, 101
Jesus, xi, 14, 53, 108, 109, 111, 115, 119, 123, 125, 132, 133, 137, 140
"Jesus Gave Me Water" (Soul Stirrers), vii
John 4:16, xiii

Johnson, Robert, 127
Jungian psychology, xi

King James Bible, 37
King, Carole, 135-36
King, Martin Luther, Jr., 133034
King, Stephen, 71
Knightley, Keira, 73
Kristofferson, Kris, 135

La India, 132
La Lupe, 132
Lanier (Bassano), Emilia, 41
Last Judgment, The (Michelangelo), 13
Lawrence, D.H., 61, 78
Leah (Bible), 51
Lee, Ang, 78
Lefroy, Tom, 80
Legend, John, 136
lesbianism, 71, 84
Lethe, 24
"Let's Get It On" (Marvin Gaye), 139
"Letter, The" (Box Tops), 135
Lewis, C.S., ix
Li, Jet, 58
libido, ix, 47, 51, 91, 106, 107, 109, 129, 140
"Light My Fire" (Doors), 137
Lion King, The, 58
Little Book of Atheist Spirituality, The (Comte-Sponville), xi
Locke, John, 41
Longfellow, Henry Wadsworth, 1
Lorde, Audre, 126

Luke, Gospel of, 53, 122
lust, ix, 14, 16, 20, 21, 35, 43, 45, 46, 47, 59, 64, 66, 137

Macfadyen, Matthew, 73
Machito, 132
MacIntyre, Alisdair, 77
Mann, Thomas, 2
Mansfield Park (See Austen, Jane, Works)
March on Washington, 134
Marlowe, Christopher, 2, 40, 41, 61
marriage, 48, 72, 74, 80-83, 85, 89, 96, 97, 99, 100, 110
Mary, Queen of England, 39
masturbation, 84
Matthew, Gospel of, 22, 53
Mayfield, Curtis, 133
McCartney, Paul, 5
Measure for Measure (See Shakespeare, William, Works)
Merton, Thomas, xi
Methodism, 93
Michelangelo, 5, 13
Midsummer Night's Dream, A (See Shakespeare, William, Works)
misogyny, 42
Mitchell, Willie, 114, 115, 116, 117, 136, 138
Moses, 121, 133
Murray, Albert, 128
"My Girl" (Temptations), vii

Nelson, Willie, 130, 135
Newman, John, 130
Newton, Isaac, 41

"No More Auction Block for Me," 133
Norris, Kathleen, 95

Olatunji, 132
O., 42
objectification, 42
"Old Time Religion," 116
Olivier, Laurence, 73
Original sin, 10
Othello (See Shakespeare, William, Works)
Out to Lunch (Potter), 1
Oxford English Dictionary, 37

Paltrow, Gwyneth, 40
Paradise (see also Heaven), x, xi, 4, 6, 7, 9, 11, 13, 23, 24, 25-31, 77, 101, 106, 107, 109, 110, 111, 116, 118, 121, 130, 131, 135, 138, 139, 140
Paster, Gail Kern, 61
patriarchy, 56, 57, 62, 66, 74, 77, 78
Paz, Octavio, ix
Pembroke, Earl of, 41
Pentacostalism, 121, 122, 131, 132
Petrarch, 59
philia, ix, xi, 3, 5, 39, 54, 72, 75; defined, viii; Dante and, 4; in *Divine Comedy*, 4, 12, 16, 17, 20, 22, 23, 25, 27-31; Shakespeare and, 37, 38; in *Othello*, 42, 43, 46; in *Measure for Measure*, 47-50, 52; in *A Midsummer Night's Dream*, 57; in *Romeo and Juliet*, 58, 59, 62-64; in

Antony and Cleopatra, 64, 65; Jane Austen and, 72, 77; in *Pride and Prejudice*, 82, 83, 85, 86; in *Mansfield Park*, 88, 90, 91, 93; in *Emma*, 97, 98, 100, 101; Al Green and, 106, 107, 110-12; in Al Green's music, 115, 129, 131-32, 133, 135-36
Pinsky, Robert, 5
Playboy philosophy, The, 86
Poe, Edgar Allan, 71
Point of It All, The (Anthony Hamilton), 137
Potter, Susan, 1
prayer, 18, 19, 60, 62, 135
"Precious Lord Take My Hand" (Aretha Franklin), 135
Presley, Elvis, 130
Pride and Prejudice (See Austen, Jane, Works)
Pride and Prejudice (film, 1940), 73
Pride and Prejudice (film, 2005), 73
Pride and Prejudice and Zombies, 71
Pride and Promiscuity: The Lost Sex Scenes of Jane Austen, 84
Prince (musician), 61
Prokofiev, Serge, 58
Protestantism, 76
Purgatory, xii, 4, 7, 9, 16, 17-22, 23, 25, 31, 63, 71, 72, 76, 77, 92, 93, 94, 98, 99, 100, 101, 102, 136

Quakerism, xi

Rachel (Bible), 5
racism, 42
Rae, Corinne Bailey, 136
Rebel Without a Cause, 58
redemption, 45, 46, 111, 128, 133, 139
Reed, Lou, 58
Reformation, The, 76
repentance, 4, 7, 16, 18, 19, 21, 23, 24, 25, 94-100
repression, x, xi, xii, xiii, 47, 48, 65, 72, 79, 84, 91, 94, 96, 124
Rice, Anne, 71
Rich, Adrienne, 115
Robinson, Smokey, 5
Rolling Stone magazine, 118
Romeo and Juliet (See Shakespeare, William, Works)
Roots, The, 136
Rosetti, Dante Gabriel, 5
Royal Scots Dragoon Guards, 130

salsa music, 132
salvation, 123
samba music, 132
Sampson, George, 78
Sartre, Jean-Paul, 92
Satan (see also Devil), 2, 9, 19, 46
Saving Private Ryan, 40
seduction, 89, 130
Sense and Sensibility (film), 78
Sense and Sensibility and Sea Serpents, 71
sensuality, 59, 65, 66
seven deadly sins, 8, 66, 100
seven social sins, 8
Sex and the City, 126
Shakespeare, William, xi, xii,

35-68, 76, 79, 80, 81, 90, 99, 119, 126, 128, 139; and English language, 37; and Southampton, 38; and London, 38, 40; and Catholicism, 39; and Elizabethan theater, 39; life of, 40; biographical speculations, 40, 41; erotic life of, 41; marriage, 41 British "Person of the Millennium," 41

Works

Antony and Cleopatra, 36, 64-68, 132; Cleopatra's erotic intelligence, 64; clash of Rome, Egypt, 65-66; patriarchy in, 66; Cleopatra as performer, 66-67; political theater in, 67; death of Cleopatra, 67

As You Like It, 37, 81, 102

Hamlet, 56, 128

Macbeth, 56

Measure for Measure, 47-54, 63; plot, 47-48; fornication theme, 48; mercy in, 48-49, 53; Isabella's decision, 50; Claudio's plea, 51; resolution, 51-52, 53; bed trick in, 51; significance of title, 53

Midsummer Night's Dream, A, 38, 54-58, 61, 102; plot strands, 54-55; erotic violence in, 55-56; Green World in, 56; patriarchy in, 56; creative imagination in, 57; happy ending of, 57; dreams in, 57

Othello, 35, 42-47, 54, 99; modern versions of, 42; lust in, 43; Desdemona's handkerchief, 43-44; feminist perspective in, 44-45; Hell in, 45; Virtue in, 45; murder of Desdemona, 46; conclusion of, 46-47

Rape of Lucrece, The, 38

Richard II, 39

Romeo and Juliet, 35, 40, 41, 58-64, 99, 126; as comedy, 37, 58; modern adaptations, 58; Romeo's infatuation, 59; lust in, 59; first meeting of Romeo and Juliet, 60; Juliet's realism 60-61; commodification of women, 61; organized religion in, 62; wedding of Romeo and Juliet, 62; images of Hell, 63; Tybalt's death, 63

Sonnet 20, 38

Sonnet 129, 35

Sonnet 138, 35, 36

Twelfth Night, 37

Venus and Adonis, 38

Characters

Angelo (*Measure*), 48-53; Antony, 64-68; Benvolio (*Romeo*), 59; Bottom, Nick, 54, 55, 57; Caesar (*Antony and Cleopatra*), 64-68; Cassio (*Othello*), 43-, 44, 46; Claudio (*Measure*), 48-52, 54; Cleopatra, 37, 64-67; Demetrius (*Midsummer*), 55-56, 64; Desdemona, 42-47; Duke of Vienna (*Measure*), 47, 48, 51-54; Egeus (*Midsummer*), 55-57, 61;

Emilia (*Othello*), 42, 44, 45, 46, 47; Enobarbus, 37, 64, 65; Eros (*Antony and Cleopatra*), 68; Falstaff, 54; Friar Laurence, 62-63; Helena (*Midsummer*), 55; Hermia (*Midsummer*), 55-56; Hippolyta (*Midsummer*), 55-57; Iago, 42-47; Isabella (*Measure*), 48-54, 64; Juliet 37, 59-63, 64; Julietta (*Measure*), 48-50; Lucio (*Measure*), 48, 49, 52; Lysander (*Midsummer*), 55-56; Mercutio, 37, 59-61; Oberon (*Midsummer*), 54-57; Ophelia, 94; Othello, 42-47, 99; Puck, 54-57; Romeo, 58-63; Rosaline (*Romeo and Juliet*), 59, 61; Theseus (*Midsummer*), 55-56; Titania (*Midsummer*), 55-57; Tybalt, 37, 61, 63
Shakespeare in Love, 40, 41, 58, 80
shame, 24, 66
Shulamite, The, 28
sin, 4, 8, 9, 10, 19, 21, 24-25, 26, 49, 50, 60, 62, 66, 93, 95, 97, 99, 100, 105, 123, 127, 129, 133, 139
slavery, 111, 122, 130, 132
Solomon, King, 28
"Something" (Beatles), 135
Song of Songs, 28, 29, 126
soul music, x, 111, 112, 113, 118, 139
"Soul Serenade," 114
Soul Stirrers, The, vii, 118
Southampton. Countess of, 41

Southampton, Earl of, 38, 39, 41
Spence, Jon, 80
Spencer, Scott, 123
Spielberg, Stephen, 40
spirituals, 111, 133
Springsteen, Bruce, 58
Staple Singers, 116
Staples, Mavis, 133
storge, ix
suicide, 8, 14, 109
Supremes, The, 58

Talmud, 9
Taoism, xi
Tapestry (Carole King), 135
Tchaikovsky, 58
Te Deum, 17
Temptations, The, vii, 118
Thompson, Questlove, 117, 136-37
Tillich, Paul, 14
Trinity (see also God, Jesus and Holy Spirit), 31, 121
Truth Universally Acknowledged: 33 Great Writers on Why We Read Jane Austen, A, 78
Twain, Mark, 78
Two Guys Read Jane Austen, 78

Victoria, Queen, 41

Waits, Tom, 58
Wells, H.G., 78
West Side Story, 58
White, Tony Joe, 42
Whitman, Walt, 21, 54, 61
Williams, Hank, 137

Wilson, Jackie, 112, 113
Wollstonecraft, Mary, 41
Wonder, Stevie, 133
Woodson, Mary, 105, 106, 108, 109
Woolf, Leonard, 79
Woolf, Virginia, 79
Wright, Richard, 127
Wriothesley, Henry (see Southampton, Earl of)
Wriothesley, Elizabeth (see Southampton, Countess of)

Yeats, William Butler, 115
"Yesterday," 10
"You Really Got a Hold on Me," 10
"You've Got a Friend" (Aretha Franklin), 135-36